GRANDP...

# ROBOTS
## AND THE WHOLE TECHNOLOGY STORY

Glenn Murphy wrote his first book, *Why Is Snot Green?*, while working at the Science Museum, London. Since then he has written around twenty popular-science titles aimed at kids and teens, including the bestselling *How Loud Can You Burp?* and *Space: The Whole Whizz-Bang Story*.

These days he lives in sunny, leafy North Carolina – with his wife Heather, his son Sean, and two *unfeasibly* large felines.

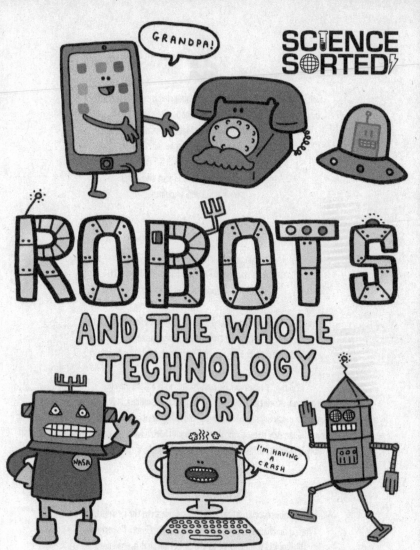

SCIENCE SORTED

GRANDPA!

I'M HAVING A CRASH

# ROBOTS
## AND THE WHOLE TECHNOLOGY STORY

# GLENN MURPHY

Illustrated by Mike Phillips

MACMILLAN CHILDREN'S BOOKS

Some material in this book has previously been published in 2011
by Macmillan Children's Books in Robots, Chips and Techno Stuff
This edition published 2015 by Macmillan Children's Books
an imprint of Pan Macmillan
20 New Wharf Road, London N1 9RR
Associated companies throughout the world
www.panmacmillan.com

ISBN 978-1-4472-8487-1

Text copyright © Glenn Murphy 2011, 2015
Illustrations copyright © Mike Phillips 2011, 2015
Design and doodles: Dan Newman

The right of Glenn Murphy and Mike Phillips to be identified as the
author and illustrator of this work has been asserted by them
in accordance with the Copyright, Designs and Patents Act 1988.

35798642

A CIP catalogue record for this book is available from the British Library.
Printed and bound in Germany by GGP Media GmbH, Poessneck

# CONTENTS

# WHAT'S THE BIG DEAL ABOUT COMPUTERS?

What's the big deal? The big deal is that you live in an incredible, super-charged, super-connected digital world that your grandparents could never have dreamed of. But do you know how it all works?

**Course I do. You just switch on the computer, click the app or browser thingy, and . . .** Okay, so maybe you know how to use computers, but do you know how to fix one or build one? If someone asked you to, could you design a robot, a smartphone or a 3DTV?

**Well, if you put it that way . . . err . . . no. I s'pose not.**

Here are some even simpler ones for you: *what is a robot?* And *what is a computer?*

Easy! A robot is like a big, metal . . . err . . . person, and a computer's like an electronic notepad with . . . well . . . you type on it, and there's a screen and windows and apps and stuff, and . . . (sigh). Maybe it's not that easy after all.

Wouldn't you like to know the answers to those questions?

## I bought this book, didn't I?
Good point.

## Go on, then.
Right – first up: **robots**. In short, a **robot** is a machine that **does things for humans**. Often boring, difficult or dangerous **work** that humans *could* do, but really rather wouldn't. Some robots look like humans, or mimic human movements. But many don't. In fact, most robots look nothing like humans, and move more like snakes, insects or other animals.

*The word robot actually comes from the Czech word robota, meaning 'worker' or 'slave'. So robots are basically electromechanical slaves built to serve their human masters. Bwahahahahaa! Ahem.*

3

## Really? Robot snakes and insects?

Yep – more about those later. For now, it's enough to know this: right now, there are *millions* of robots in the world, doing *millions* of tough, tricky jobs – on land, on sea, underground and even underwater. And to *build* a working robot . . . well . . . motors, batteries and body parts are not enough. You also need to give it some sort of electronic brain or controller. That's where **computers** come in.

## Okay, then – so what's a computer, and how do you build one of those?

A computer is any device that helps humans to deal with (or make sense of) information. They get their name from the word *compute*, which means *to add up*. This is because the earliest computers were simple counting tools, used to do sums that were too tricky for humans to do easily in their heads. Over time, these developed into modern computers, which are electronic machines that not only help us make sense of numbers, but also of patterns, pictures, words, chess moves and much, much more.

## Counting machines

### The abacus

This was the earliest 'computer' (or computing device) and dates back to around 2500 BC. It was used by the mathematicians of ancient Babylonia (who lived in what is now known as Iraq). It was invented to help calculate trades between farmers, merchants and customers. Later, Chinese mathematicians and craftsmen made handy, portable abacuses using beads threaded on to wire.

## The mechanical calculator

Invented by French mathematician Blaise Pascal, in 1642, it cranked out eight-digit additions using hand-turned cogs, gears and wheels. But, amazing as it was, Pascal's machine couldn't subtract, multiply or divide – only add.

## The 'difference engine'

In 1849, English inventor Charles Babbage designed his enormously complex 'difference engine'. Babbage never lived to see his designs become reality, but the Science Museum in London built the machine according to his original plans (made up of an astonishing 25,000 individual parts). It could perform complex multiplication sums up to thirty decimal places and had many of the basic elements of modern computers, including a memory, a processor and switchable functions or programs.

# Size matters

The valves and switches that went into the first electronic computers were much bigger than the microscopic circuits we use today. This made the computers themselves pretty chunky as a result. Check out these bad boys. In their time, these computers were about the smallest and best you could get. Good thing they've come on a bit . . .

| Computer | Year | Memory | Weight | Size of a . . . |
|---|---|---|---|---|
| UNIVAC | 1951 | 1–9kB | 24,000 kg (53,000 lb) | Room |
| Altair 8800 | 1975 | 32–64kB | 13 kg (30 lb) | Suitcase |
| Apple Macintosh | 1984 | 128kB | 7 kg (16 lb) | Beach ball |
| Apple Powerbook | 1993 | 160MB | 3 kg (7 lb) | Cushion |
| Apple Macbook Air | 2010 | 256GB | 1 kg (2.2 lb) | Notepad |

*Computer memory is measured in the number of bytes of information it can hold. A byte is equal to eight bits of digital information. For bigger memory banks a Kilobyte (kB) is a thousand bytes, a Megabyte (MB) is a million bytes and a Gigabyte (GB) is a trillion bytes.*

Basically, computers *take in information* (or **input**), *work* with it (or **process** it) and then *churn it out* again in a more useful form, as **output**. In the very simplest computers, that's pretty much the end of the story. In more complex computers, the **output** becomes another **input**, and the information goes through the **input-output** cycle thousands and thousands of times before the final output pops out. But the idea is pretty much the same. Computers **process inputs into useful outputs.** That's it.

Now to build a computer, you obviously need *things to input with* (like a **keyboard** or a **touchscreen**), *things to output with* (like a **screen** or **printer**) and *things to store and process information with* (like **memory drives** and one or more **Central Processing Units**). Together, all this stuff is known as **hardware.**

**If you were to open up an average home computer, here's what you'd find inside:**

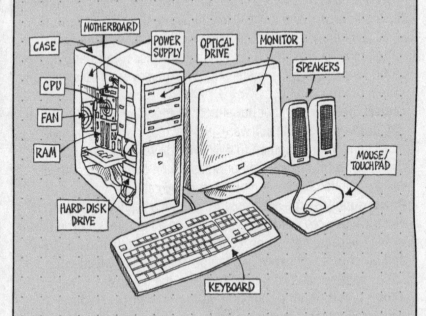

**Motherboard** - a big, printed circuit-board about the size of an A4 sketch pad. This provides a handy base for most of the computer's essential parts, along with connectors for input and output devices like monitors and keyboards.

**CPU** - the microprocessor that forms the core of the computer. This sits within a little frame on the motherboard, usually with a small, box-like fan on top. Microchips heat up quite a bit as they work, so the fan is needed to keep them from overheating.

**RAM** - (random access memory) - another chip on the motherboard, which stores information temporarily while the computer is running. This type of memory has no moving parts, so can transfer information very quickly. But it is erased every time you switch your computer off.

**Hard-disk drive (or HDD)** – your computer's permanent memory bank. This contains the computer's operating system program (e.g. Windows) along with all other programs, text documents, pictures, video files and music files. It sits in its own box, separate from the motherboard and looks like a miniature CD player – with a small, spinning disc in the middle which is scanned rapidly by a little moving arm. When it's running, the disc rotates at over 7,000 revolutions per minute, and the arm moves so quickly it's little more than a blur.

**Optical drive** – most (but not all) computers have CD, DVD or Blu-Ray drives for loading software, playing music, movies and games, and saving information on to disk. Disk drives sit in their own little box (with the disk tray or slot sticking out of the computer casing), connected to the motherboard by cables.

**Power supply** – a power transformer which supplies power to all electrical devices inside the computer. In a PC, this is a little box inside the computer casing, connected to the motherboard, drives and other parts by wires. In a laptop, the box sits outside the main computer, and is used to recharge the battery.

**Fans** – fans inside the computer casing keep the warm air generated inside moving through, which keeps components cool and prevents damage from overheating.

**Case** – this is just a big box (usually plastic, but it can be made of anything from aluminium to bamboo) that surrounds the computer's components. It contains everything we've already mentioned.

**Keyboard** – used to input characters and program the computer. Attaches to the motherboard via a cable in most PCs, but some are connected by wireless (Bluetooth or infrared) transmitters and receivers. In a laptop, the keyboard sits right on top of the motherboard.

*For this reason, spilling water or juice over your laptop may destroy the whole computer, whereas spilling it over a PC keyboard will only damage the keyboard itself.*

**Monitor** – output device used to display characters, images and video onscreen. Attaches to the casing and motherboard via cables.

**Mouse/touchpad** – input devices used to control onscreen cursors, select icons and scroll text.

**Speakers** – amplify sounds, music and video audio tracks. In a laptop, these may be built into the casing; in a PC, they are often separate. They are connected to sounds circuits on the motherboard.

**Modem** – a set of components (either on the motherboard or connected to it) found in most computers that allow it to send and receive information via digital phone lines and wireless Internet connections.

# Hold on a minute. What was that about microchips? They sound tasty.

A microchip isn't a snack, but you will find them in the belly of every computer. A microchip is a **miniaturized electronic circuit** that forms the core of all modern computers. It wasn't until the invention of microchips – thin wafers of *silicon* stamped with tiny electronic circuits – that more powerful (and less massive!) computers became possible.

For this reason, people used to call them 'silicon chips'.

# Computer Bits and Pieces

Can you match the computer parts on the left to the jobs and functions on the right? I've done the first one for you. See how many you can get. Answers on page 132.

| Part | Job |
|------|-----|
| Motherboard | used to input characters and program the computer |
| RAM | displays text, images and video onscreen |
| Mouse | the computer's core or central processing unit |
| Keyboard | controls cursor, selects icons and scrolls text |
| Monitor | creates a base for most of the computer's essential parts |
| Hard-disk drive | the computer's temporary memory bank |
| CPU | the computer's permanent memory bank |

But if all computers are built more or less the same way, then how do you get them to do so many different types of things?

Ahh, good question. That's all down to **software**. Computer software is a program or set of instructions that tells a computer what to do. Without software, a computer is just a heap of useless (but rather expensive) junk. By creating different types of software, and using it

to **program** computer hardware in different ways, you can turn a simple number-crunching machine into a handy, multipurpose tool. One you can use for everything from emailing and instant-messaging to predicting the weather and searching the skies for signs of alien life.

## Computers really do all that?

Yep. All that and more. Not only that, computers are still developing at an incredible rate. They're getting smaller, faster and more powerful every year. They're supercharging our radios, TVs, tablets and smartphones, building virtual worlds through the Internet, and leading to a whole new generation of intelligent robots and androids. This is the amazing digital world we'll be exploring in this book. We'll find out how computers 'think', we'll see how computers control our gadgets, and peek into the **future of televisions**, **audio players**, **mobile phones** and **video games**. We'll discover how the **Internet** works, and we'll explore the wide world of **robots**. We'll meet huge robots, tiny robots, pet robots, battle robots and humanlike androids that walk, talk and act just like real people.

## Whoa! Sounds like quite a ride. So where do we start?

First we'll need to learn to talk to our computers . . .

# What language does a computer speak?

Computers do not read, speak or understand languages as we know them. Instead, they read and speak in code, using only the language of logic.

## What? That doesn't make much sense.
Why's that?

## Well, all computers get **programmed**, right?
Right. Without programming, a computer can't do anything at all. It just sits there like a high-tech toaster.

## So, **someone** has to tell the computer what to do . . .
Yep. That job falls to computer engineers and programmers. A computer can only really deal with one form of information – **binary code**. This is the only language (or form of information) a computer can use.

Every bit of information inside a computer is converted into strings of 1s and 0s representing numbers, letters and commands, which then flash through computer circuits as a series of electrical pulses.

## Get It Sorted – Binary Code

Binary code is a way of representing numbers, letters and instructions as a string of 1s and 0s. For example, the letter 'a', translated into binary, is 01100001, while 'b' is 01100010, and 'z' is 01111010. Using this system, you can represent any number, word, phrase or command by sticking these strings of binary code together, like this:

| | |
|---|---|
| cat | 01100011 01100001 01110100 |
| 3 fat cats | 00110011 00100000 01100110 01100001 01110100 00100000 01100011 01100001 01110100 01110011 |
| the fat cat sat on the mat | 01110100 01101000 01100101 00100000 01100110 01100001 01110100 00100000 01100011 01100001 01110100 00100000 01110011 01100001 01110100 00100000 01101111 01101110 00100000 01110100 01101000 01100101 00100000 01101101 01100001 01110100 |

Because it only involves two characters (1 and 0), you can use binary code to turn any number, word, phrase (even pictures, video clips and pieces of music) into a series of digital, electronic signals. Think of it like switching a light bulb on and off, lots and lots of times, very, very quickly. If 'on'=1, and 'off'=0, then you can spell out any word or phrase or command just by flicking the light switch on and off in the right sequence. This, in a way, is what happens inside a computer. Only instead of light switches and light bulbs, computers use electromagnetic switches and tiny pulses of electricity.

## Wait – does that mean programmers have to learn to speak binary code?

The earliest programmers did, yes. They spent hours flicking switches on and off, or punching holes in pieces of cardboard, to create coded messages and programs that their computers could process. But before too long they realized that this method was too difficult and time-consuming for all but the simplest programming tasks.

## Bet it was seriously B-O-R-I-N-G, too.

No doubt. So, to avoid this, they came up with an easier option. Instead of learning computer-ese, they created interpreters and translators that could talk to the computers for them. First, they created new **programming languages** based on natural human language and mathematics. This gave programmers a kind of shorthand for common commands like PRINT (which told a computer to display something on the screen), and INPUT or SCAN (which told a computer to wait for input from a keyboard). Then they wrote programs (the hard way, using 1s and 0s) that could translate typed instructions like PRINT into pure binary code, automatically. With this, programmers were freed from all the switching and punching, and could input information directly into the computer as numbers and text. Over the years, as computer functions (and commands) have become more and more complex, thousands of programming languages have been designed to help translate human instructions into pure binary code. But only a handful of these are used in most modern desktops and laptops. These languages include **BASIC**, **C++**, **COBOL**, **FORTRAN** and **Java**.

## Computer Lingo

| | |
|---|---|
| **Interpreted languages** – easy to read and easy to program but limited in what they can do | **BASIC** **LISP** |
| **Compiled languages** – harder to learn, but much more powerful | **C++** **COBOL** **FORTRAN** |
| **P-code languages** – pretty fast and powerful, and fairly easy for human programmers to read, write and understand. | **Java** **Python** |

# Get It Sorted – Logic Gates

Logic gates are the building blocks of computer circuits. They take one or more binary inputs, compare the input values (1s or 0s) to each other and turn them into a single output (either a 1 or a 0). You can see a few examples of the most basic logic gates below.

**NOT** gate (turns an input of 1 into an output of 0, or vice versa)

**AND** gate (if both inputs – A and B – are 1s, then the output is 1. Otherwise, the output is 0)

**OR** gate (if either A *or* B is a 1, then the output is 1. Otherwise, the output is 0)

By linking lots of these gates together, engineers can build complex **logic arrays** inside computers that can process all kinds of complex information.

This is how today's computers turn a thousand separate temperature and pressure readings into a prediction of tomorrow's weather, or future climate change. It's how a chess computer can take 'inputs' from the arrangement of pieces on a chess board, compare them with arrangements it has 'seen' in other games and turn it all into an 'output' (like a single brilliant chess move) that checkmates a skilled human player. And it's how computers seem to be thinking, when all they're *really* doing is *processing*.

## Will we ever be able to just talk to computers, and program them that way?

One day, yes – we probably will. Right now, speech-recognition programs are mostly only used for word-processing or simple smartphone commands. Within a few decades, though, computers may start learning *our* languages, rather than the other way around. For more complex programs, engineers will probably still choose to type instructions into computers, just as they do today. For them, it'll be quicker that way. But for the rest of us voice-programming may come in quite handy. Soon, you'll be telling your computer to add a webpage to your 'favourites' list just by saying 'keep it'. You'll be sending texts and emails just by talking at your laptop or tablet. And you'll be training your pet robot by shouting 'sit!', 'stay!' and 'fetch!'.

## Now **that's** more like it!

# Geekspeak

Computer programmers learn languages like Java to talk to computers. But they also use a whole language of their own when chatting to each other. Abbreviations like LOL, OMG and THX have now made their way into text messages and IMs the world over. But what about these? See how many you can guess correctly. Answers on page 132.

**1. ROFL means**
a) Rolling On the Floor, Laughing
b) Running Out For Lunch
c) Rolling Ostrich Feathers Lightly

**2. NT means:**
a) Nice Tan
b) No Time
c) No, Thanks

**3) a chip head is:**
a) Part of a microprocessor chip
b) Someone who is really into computers
c) Someone who likes fish 'n' chips

**4) a screamer is:**
a) a fast computer
b) a fast programmer
c) a broken loudspeaker

**5) a n00b is:**
a) a type of wireless mouse
b) someone who knows a lot about computers
c) someone new to computing or gaming; a newbie

# SIGNALS, CODES AND SMARTPHONES

## How did people talk before telephones?

Before modern telephones, staying in touch long-distance was very tricky. There were many ways to do it, including runners, riders, flags and fires. But these 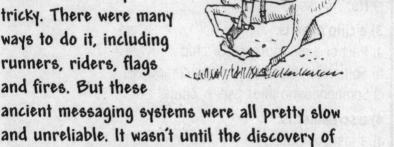 ancient messaging systems were all pretty slow and unreliable. It wasn't until the discovery of electricity – and the invention of the telegraph – that truly 'instant' messages became possible.

Wow. That all sounds pretty complicated. But what if you had to get a message to someone, like, right away?

Well, for the most part you just couldn't, people just accepted that it took days, months or years to get messages about. And that's how it stayed right up until the nineteenth century.

## What happened then?

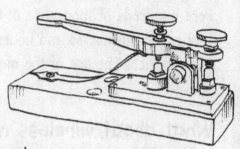

In 1837, the electric telegraph was invented by British engineers William Cooke and Charles Wheatstone. This used a system of magnetic coils to send messages through wires in the form of an electric current. To use a telegraph, you had to learn a whole new language – a system of coded knocks, taps or beeps later known as Morse Code (named after American inventor Samuel Morse, who improved upon the design of Cooke and Wheatstone's telegraph). Trained telegraph operators had to tap messages out at one end of the wire and decode them into written words at the other.

## Sounds a bit tricky.

It was. But it was the best thing they had. It wasn't until 1876 that long-distance messaging got a bit more user-friendly. Three engineers – Antonio Meucci, Elisha Gray and Alexander Graham Bell – all invented types of electric telephone. All three were based upon the idea of using a magnet to convert the human voice into a series of electric signals, which could then be sent through wires just like telegraphs. But it was Bell's telephone design that eventually caught on. By the late 1800s, there were hundreds of thousands of Bell's electric telephones connecting businesses and households throughout Europe and America. The age of the modern phone call had arrived.

## What about wireless networks?

Well, in 1895 Italian engineer Guglielmo Marconi built the first wireless (or radio) transmitter and receiver. Marconi's wireless telegraphs were initially used to communicate with ships out at sea, but they later evolved into two-way 'talk radios' used by military commanders, and eventually into the wireless telephone and communications networks we all enjoy today.

## Good thing, too. Wouldn't fancy texting my mates in Morse Code!

# Do It Yourself: build your own electric telegraph!

Make your own telegraph for sending secret messages between rooms. You might need help to find the bits and pieces you need at the shops. But, once you're all hooked up, you'll have your very own secret telegraph system.

## What you'll need

- 2 bits of cardboard, about 20 cm x 10 cm
- 2 more bits of cardboard, about 3 cm x 8 cm
- 3 lengths of wire, about 20 cm long
- 3 longer pieces of insulated electrical wire (long enough to trail between two rooms)
- 1 battery (D size)
- 4 drawing pins
- 2 electric buzzers (you can buy these in electrical shops)
- pencil, scissors, pliers and sticky tape

**How to do it**

**To make the first transmitter (or 'sounder'):**

1. Take one large piece of cardboard, draw a line down the centre, dividing it in half, width-ways. This will be your sounder base.

2. Take one small piece of cardboard, put a bend in it about 2 cm from one end, then tape that end to the base, close to (and parallel to) one short edge of the base. This will be your signalling switch. To complete it, push one drawing pin into the base (just beneath the free, flapping end of the switch) and the other into the underside of the flapping end above. When you press the switch down, the heads of the two drawing pins should now click together.

3. Find a spot on the opposite side of the base, and tape the buzzer there.

4. Place the battery on the line you drew in step 1, and tape it down to the base (leaving the ends free).

5. Now take one short wire, tape one end to the base (i.e. the flat end) of the battery, and connect the other end to the buzzer – twist it around one of the wires sticking out of the buzzer, and tape them together.

6. Now take the other short wire, tape one end to the battery base (make sure it's touching metal, and not just tape), wrap the other end tightly around the drawing pin. Lift up the base, look underneath, and use the pliers to

bend the tip of the pin over, so it won't slip out (get a parent to help with this).

**To make the second transmitter:**
Take the other large piece of cardboard, and repeat steps 1–3 above.
1. Take another short wire, wrap one end around the lower drawing pin (as before) and connect the other to the buzzer (wrapping and taping it, as before).
2. Place it in another room to transmitter #1.

**Now connect the two transmitters together:**
1. Take your three long wires and run them between the two rooms, placing the ends close to the two transmitters.
2. Use the first long wire to connect the buzzer of transmitter #2 to the upper pin of the switch on transmitter #1 (again, bend the end of the pin over with pliers to stop it falling out).
3. Use the second wire to connect the buzzer of transmitter #1 to the upper pin of the switch on transmitter #2.
4. Finally, use the third wire to connect the free (positive) end of the battery on transmitter #1 to the lower pin on transmitter #2.

That's it! You're done. Now you can tap out secret messages in Morse Code between the two rooms, plan secret meetings or launch your plot to take over the world. Whatever you fancy.

See overleaf for a complete Morse Code letter map to use.

# Morse Code letter map

| | | | | |
|---|---|---|---|---|
| A | ·– | P | ·––· |
| B | –··· | Q | ––·– |
| C | –·–· | R | ·–· |
| D | –·· | S | ··· |
| E | · | T | – |
| F | ··–· | U | ··– |
| G | ––· | V | ···– |
| H | ···· | W | ·–– |
| I | ·· | X | –··– |
| J | ·––– | Y | –·–– |
| K | –·– | Z | ––·· |
| L | ·–·· | Full stop | ·–·–·– |
| M | –– | Comma | ––··–– |
| N | –· | Out | ·–·–· |
| O | ––– | | (message ends) |

# How do mobile phones find each other?

They send out signals to tell their local mobile phone networks (or grids) where to find them. To connect a phone call between them, a computer-controlled exchange system lends them a pair of radio channels to chat, and bounces radio waves, microwaves and digital electronic signals back and forth as you talk.

## All that happens every time you call someone?

Yep. Every time.

## Wow. That seems like an awful lot of bother just for a quick phone call.

I suppose it is. But I guess most people (well, most mobile-phone fans, anyway) would say it was worth it. Besides it all happens so fast you don't even notice. You just dial (or select) a number, and within two or three seconds the call is connected automatically. One second later, a suitably irritating ringtone starts blaring out on your friend's phone. Provided that they pick it up, you're now ready to blather away about nothing and everything – blissfully unaware of all the switching, bouncing and beaming of electromagnetic signals that are making your conversation possible.

## Walkie-Talkie Happy Talk

HELP!

Thousands of soldiers, lorry drivers, police officers, paramedics and fire-fighters use these two-way radio systems today. Each walkie-talkie handset contains a microphone, a speaker, a battery, an antenna, and an electronic radio transmitter and receiver. To 'call' a pal with a walkie-talkie, you need to agree (before you set off) on the exact radio channel (or frequency) you will be using. Then you simply tune the radio to that channel to receive signals, and push a button to transmit (or talk back) on the same channel.

Walkie-talkies work fine if only one person needs to talk at a time. If you try to 'butt in' and talk while someone else is still transmitting, your message will either be lost altogether or (at the very least) garbled or cut off, mid-sentence. To get around this, two-way radio users have to take turns talking and use special codes to tell the listener when they've finished a message or conversation. That's why most walkie-talkie conversations sound like this:

*Shhhhhhhhhh* (click) 'Victor Alpha Tango, this is Golf Juliet Mike . . . OVER.'

*Shhhhhhhhhh* (click) 'Golf Juliet Mike, this is Victor Alpha Tango . . . hello, Glenn . . . OVER.'

*Shhhhhhhhhh* (click) 'Hello, Vicky . . . listen – can you pick up a pizza on the way home? . . . OVER.'

*Shhhhhhhhhh* (click) 'Is that it? Just a pizza? . . . OVER.'

*Shhhhhhhhhh* (click) 'Errr, no, actually . . . I've been thinking, and I don't want you to be my girlfriend any more . . . It's just too difficult going out with a police-woman . . . It's over!'

*Shhhhhhhhhh* (click) 'I'm sorry . . . it's – what? OVER.'

*Shhhhhhhhhh* (click) 'I said "it's over" . . . OVER.'

*Shhhhhhhhhh* (click) 'What do you mean, "it's over-over"? You're not making any sense . . . OVER.'

*Shhhhhhhhhh* (click) 'No, no, no . . . not "over-over". Just "over" . . . As in "we're finished" . . . or "I want to break up with you" . . . OVER.'

*Shhhhhhhhhh* (click) 'Oh . . . . well in that case, you can get your own pizza. OVER AND OUT.'

Modern mobile phones use a *pair* of radio channels (or frequencies) to communicate back and forth. When a call is placed, and two mobile phones are connected, they are automatically assigned (or tuned to) a pair of radio frequencies – one to send, one to receive. So each phone can transmit and receive simultaneously, and the speakers are free to butt in whenever they like, without fear of cutting each other off. (And they can forget about all that irritating 'OVER' stuff.)

# Police Codes Wordsearch

When police officers call in number plates and soldiers radio map positions to each other, they use special words to represent the letters of the alphabet, so that they're not misheard or misunderstood. This is called the Phonetic Alphabet. 'AB1 GHC', for example, would be said 'Alpha Bravo one, Golf Hotel Charlie'. Learn the system for yourself by solving all the clues in this wordsearch puzzle. Answers on page 133.

| | | | | |
|---|---|---|---|---|
| Alpha | Bravo | Charlie | Delta | Echo |
| Foxtrot | Golf | Hotel | India | Juliet |
| Kilo | Lima | Mike | November | Oscar |
| Papa | Quebec | Romeo | Sierra | Tango |
| Uniform | Victor | Whisky | X-ray | Yankee |
| Zulu | | | | |

```
T U K M U U O F V M R R C H A R L I E T
K U A X Z U L U D I T S E E G A L Q N O
E M B Z D N O X V Z M G B I I G T N O J
A P A P S I E R R A K M E X M E H L V S
L L R M K F X W O O D N U D R O G I E F
P E N G A O H R E C H O Q O T D Y R M D
H A Z K E R L M O G N A T E S T N Y B K
A V J R B M O A B A H C L O E C M L E X
S U E M V R I J D D I J I V R Z A P R V
R M X Z K K A K N V N W M L Q T L R V G
A G F R G U I V E Y D F A A E T X R A Y
J Z F O X Z J L O O I Q N A T Y U O T P
J U L I E T Z Y O W A Y V P A H W R F Q
K F W H I S K Y Y A N K E E E E Q I G Q Z
```

## Okay, but what about all that switching and bouncing you talked about at the beginning?

That's done for two reasons. The first is to prevent interference from other callers, and the second is to keep the signal clear and strong.

In each mobile phone **network**, there's usually a single, **main exchange** in every major city. But to get a clear signal to areas outside the city the main exchange is connected to a number of local exchanges, which boost call transmissions and relay them on to local antennas (or 'cell towers'). These towers are dotted all over the landscape, and together divide it up into a grid of invisible, overlapping circles (or cells).

When you place a call each phone sends a radio signal to its nearest cell tower (this happens continuously while your phone is switched on, whether you're making a call or not). From there, the radio signals are transferred (usually as an electric signal, through an underground

This, of course, is why mobile phones are also known as 'cellphones'. Not because you're allowed to use them in prison or something.

cable) to their local exchanges, which in turn relay the signal onward (via cables or microwave transmitters) to a central main exchange, often in a neighbouring city. In this way, the main exchange can keep track of where everybody's phone is, all the time. When a call is placed, a signal is relayed from one phone to the main exchange, which locates the other phone (which, as we've just learned, is constantly 'pinging' the main exchange from local cells), assigns a pair of frequencies for them to communicate over and connects them up in the middle. From that point on, signals are relayed between cells, towers and exchanges as radio waves, microwaves and pulses of electricity.

*In fact, police detectives, spies and nosy parents with the right equipment can 'trace' your location this way – and find out where you are just by following your mobile phone signal!*

## Microwaves? Yikes! Is that why some people think that mobile phones melt your brain?

Part of it, yes.

## Do they?

Not as far as we know, no. For one thing, mobile phones don't actually emit microwaves. While mobile phone exchanges (i.e. local and central exchange towers) do communicate this way, mobiles use **low frequency radio waves**. Radio waves are a form of **non-ionizing radiation**, which means that (unlike X-rays and ultraviolet rays), they can't break through the skin, penetrate your cells or damage the DNA inside. And while mobile phones fall somewhere between TVs and microwaves in the *type* of radiation they chuck out, they operate at **tiny power levels** (around 1 watt – or about a hundredth the power of a bright home light bulb) and emit only **tiny amounts** of radiation. Also – if you think about it – **hundreds of millions** of people have been using mobile phones for **decades**, now. Yet most scientific studies have revealed **no effect** at all on the brains of mobile phone users. So, while we can't know for certain that cellphones do no damage at all, we can be fairly sure that they don't actually *melt your brain*.

Drat. Guess I'll have to find another excuse for not doing my maths homework, then. Come to think of it – does **maths** melt your brain? It certainly feels like it . . .

## What makes smartphones so smart?

In short: microchips, operating systems and downloadable programs (or applications - 'apps' for short). A modern smartphone is a super-versatile digital toolbox, which can be used for everything from homework and hobbies to push-ups and zit-popping.

## A smartphone could do my homework? All right!

Well . . . no smartphone is smart enough to do your homework *for* you. At least not yet. But they *can* help you get it done. Need to Google the population of Turkmenistan while you're sitting on the bus? Done. Need help plotting a graph for maths class? No problem. Need to translate something from English into Spanish? Too easy. Forgotten which bit of homework was due in first? There's an 'app' for that, too.

## But how can they do all that stuff? I mean, a smartphone is basically just a fancy mobile phone, right?

The early ones were, perhaps. But today's smartphones are far more than that. The first mobile phones were just two-way, wireless communication devices. Soon, they featured cameras, audio players and the ability to surf the Web. But modern smartphones are the digital equivalent of a Swiss Army knife – they come in handy for all sorts of things. With a smartphone, you can make video calls, browse any website, update your blog or Twitter feed, play games online, get directions using the global positioning system (GPS), watch movies, buy music, even scan your fingerprints. What's more, smartphones are user-programmable. New uses and applications (or apps) are being written by software programmers all the time, which can be downloaded and installed to make your smartphone even more useful.

## So smartphones are smart because you can reprogram them to do new things?

Exactly.

## In that case, what's the difference between a smartphone and a computer?

That's a good question. For a while now, smartphones have been skating the thin line between 'fancy phone' and 'pocket computer'. Now, it seems, that line has disappeared altogether. Smartphones, essentially, are pocket personal computers. You've only got to peek inside one to see it. Just like a desktop or notebook, inside a smartphone you'll find:

**1) Microprocessor chips**. These are similar to those used in most computers, only a bit smaller, simpler and less powerful. This helps to save battery power (and weight).

**2) Input devices**. Smartphones have fold/flip out keypads or high-sensitivity touchscreens. They also have a high resolution, digital camera built into them which functions as a photo camera, a video camera or a webcam

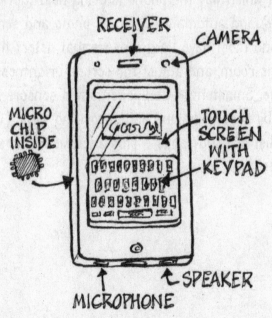

for video-calling. Plus, of course, all smartphones have built-in microphones for voice transmission and sound recording.

**3) Output devices**. Here, computer monitors and speakers are replaced with micro-speakers and small screen displays.

**4) Operating systems**. Just as desktops and notebooks use operating systems (OSs) such as Windows and OS X, smartphones have simpler mini-systems such as Android (for Google phones) and iOS (for iPhones).

Aside from these main parts, many smartphones contain a host of other sensors. These include accelerometers that detect which way the phone is being held (upright or sideways) and automatically rotate photo and screen displays. And most have light sensors that detect the light levels in the room, and adjust the screen brightness to compensate. Smartphone components and sensors are also used by apps in unique and surprising ways. (To see my Top 5 list of handy apps – plus a few weird ones – see page 44).

## So, if smartphones have turned into computers, won't they have to find a new name for them?

Maybe so. As smartphones continue to evolve, they get further and further from traditional telephones. So eventually, we will almost certainly have to come up with another name for them. The word 'phone' means 'sound' or 'voice'. Yet many smartphone users hardly *talk* at all – they spend far more time texting, web-surfing, gaming, Facebooking and Twittering. But no one has yet managed to find a name that sticks.

## How about 'smarty-box'? Or 'magical electrothingy'?

Errr . . . yeah. We'll get back to you on that one . . .

# Top 5 handiest smartphone apps

**1. My Homework** – organizes all your homework assignments on a calendar, and displays them in order of which one is due in first.

**2. Wikibuddy** – basically Wikipedia in your pocket. Great for looking up people, places and historical events.

**3. Mensa Brain Test** – test (and retest) your IQ with a tricky collection of brain teasers.

**4. Word Lens** – translates English into Spanish (other European languages are available) and vice versa, just by pointing your phone's camera at it.

**5. StarWalk** – a pocket astronomy guide that helps you identify stars, planets, satellites, constellations (and space stations!) in the night sky.

# ... and the Top 5 strangest ones

1. **iNap@work** – makes clicking, crumpling and typing noises while you nap at your desk, to make teachers, coworkers or bosses think you're working.
2. **Goggle Eyes** – a googly-eyed cartoon monkey stares blankly at you, and tracks your eye movements using facial recognition software to check that you are staring blankly back.
3. **Hello, Cow** – just a picture of a cow. You touch it, and it goes 'moo'. Weird.
4. **Pointless Game** – exactly what it sounds like. Includes tasks such as 'put a finger anywhere on the screen, and leave it there. Earn 1 point for every second you don't lift it up.'
5. **Pull My Finger/iFart** – two separate apps that serve the same essential function – annoying your teachers. They offer a range of realistic fart sounds, from 'trouser cough' to 'thermonuclear explosion'.

# ELECTRO-TAINMENT

## How can you stuff 10,000 songs into one little pocket music player?

Because when songs are converted to audio tracks, thousands of tiny, barely audible chunks are cut out of each sound file. This allows an entire album of songs to be squeezed into ten to twelve times less digital space, and an entire music collection to fit almost weightlessly in your pocket.

## What? You can get weightless audio players now? How does that work? Are they anti-gravity or something?

No, audio *players* aren't weightless. Small and light as they are, most still weigh a couple of grams, at least. But the audio files recorded on them are weightless.

So it doesn't matter if your music collection totals ten songs, a hundred songs, or 10,000 songs – you can now get it all into one tiny device, and carry it around with you all day.

# Music players - a weighty story

| Format | Songs | Weight of 10,000 songs | Weight equivalent |
|--------|-------|------------------------|-------------------|
| Vinyl records (aka 'LPs', short for long-playing records; aka 'records') | Ten to fifteen songs each so it would take about 1,000 of them to hold a full collection of 10,000 songs. | As each record weighed 200 grams, your whole collection would weigh about 200 kg. | Fully grown polar bear |
| Audio cassette tapes (aka 'tapes') | Around 20 songs per tape, so 10,000 songs would fit on 500 tapes | Each tape weighed around 80 grams, so your collection would weigh 40 kg | Your own bodyweight (roughly) |

| Compact discs (aka 'CDs') | 10,000 songs would fit on no more than 1,000 CDs | A CD weighs just 15 grams, so the whole lot would weigh 15 kg | A big, heavy bag of potatoes |
|---|---|---|---|
| Minidiscs (aka 'MDs') | With 5 times the storage space of a CD, 10,000 songs would fit on only 200 minidiscs | Minidiscs weigh about the same as CDs, but you only need 200 of them, so total weight would be 3 kg | A bag of sugar |
| iPod | 10,000 songs can fit on a single iPod | An iPod Touch weighs just 88 grams | A pot of yogurt |

Minidiscs didn't last very long – at least not for music storage. MDs are still used to store computer data in some places.

# But why? How?

Ahhh – that's all down to **digital compression**. Basically, when you convert digital music recordings into audio files, a special computer program uses clever tricks to remove large chunks of the sound without us noticing.

## So it removes whole verses or instruments? That doesn't sound so great . . .

No, not quite. It's a bit cleverer than that. Every sound recording, you see, contains a range of sounds we can't even hear, which are outside the range of human hearing. By lopping those sounds off, the audio-file-converting program saves a little space, and makes the audio file a little smaller (in terms of information, not song length!). Then it seeks out parts of the song where one instrument, singer or note is so much louder than the others that it drowns out all the rest. Since you can't really hear these background notes and sounds anyway, the program happily removes those, too. Bingo – more space saved. Using tricks like this, an original recording can be cut down (or **compressed**) until it's ten to twelve times smaller, and you'll hardly hear the difference in the audio file that comes out at the other end.

## So how are the files stored inside the audio player – on tiny discs or something?

Some do that, yes. Hard-disk audio players (like the original iPod) have small **microdisk hard-drives** inside them, which whirr and spin away as they transfer and play back your music files. These have lots of memory, and are great for storing entire music collections. But most digital audio players around today are flash-memory players. Instead of moving parts and mini-hard-drives, they contain solid computer chips that store information much like the RAM memory chips inside a desktop or

Unless, that is, you're an **audiophile** (someone who loves sound or music). With expensive music players and headphones, you'll easily tell the difference between the same song played back on a vinyl record, a CD and a compressed audio file like an mp3. Vinyl and CD recordings sound much 'fuller' and richer than compressed audio files. But most people don't know or care what they're missing, and use compressed audio anyway.

laptop. While these can't hold as much information as a hard-drive, they're smaller, lighter and have fewer moving parts. So they allow audio players to be built much smaller, or even placed inside smartphones. Thanks to audio file compression and flash drives, you can now store not just music, but also video clips and movies. This is what powers multipurpose smartphones and portable tablets like the iPad.

For more about RAM and computer memory, see 'What's the big deal about computers?' on page 2.

## Wow. I wonder what's coming next?
Who knows? But one thing's for sure – we've come a long way from plastic records.

# Get It Sorted – E-books vs Paper books

| E-books | Paper books |
|---|---|
| Most e-reader devices are less bulky and heavy than hardback books (the ones with big, thick covers) | E-readers aren't much easier to hold or carry than an average-sized paperback (thin-cover) books |
| You can cram over a thousand e-books into an e-reader – a thousand paperbacks would weigh about half a tonne! | Why would you want to carry 1,000 books around with you? Even on a month-long trip you'd have a job getting through more than ten or twelve books |
| E-books don't require paper, so you don't have to chop down rainforests to make them | It takes an enormous amount of energy (not to mention water, plastic and rare metals) to build e-reader devices |

Over the next ten or twenty years, e-books will begin to replace paper books entirely in schools, universities and other places. With fewer and fewer paper books sold, old-style bookshops (as in, the ones you actually walk into) will start disappearing. Many traditional libraries will close down, too, as even the oldest books are scanned, turned into e-books and stored in vast, electronic 'e-libraries' containing billions of volumes.

Some traditional libraries would probably be kept to store 'hard-copy' backups of books. It takes a pretty serious fire to destroy an entire library building. But with millions of books stored in one digital memory bank a single computer-crash could wipe out thousands of years' worth of knowledge in seconds.

Do you prefer reading e-books or paper books? How are you reading this right now?

# If you can download movies off the Internet, then what's the point in DVDs?

That's a very good question. Everything has to be stored somewhere, and DVDs are just one way of storing and ferrying video information. But their time will soon be up.

With the rise of Internet movies, DVDs could soon be following dinosaurs and dodos into the sad, lonely dustbin of history.

## Really?
## DVD movies are about to go extinct?

Not yet, but soon. Thanks to online movie libraries, they're definitely an endangered species.

## Get It Sorted – DVDs and HDDs

| Digital Video Disc | Hard-disk drive |
| --- | --- |
| Invented in the mid-1990s as a way of storing images, moving images (or video) and other types of digital information | Inside, hard-disk drives (or HDDs) look a bit like mini DVD players - complete with spinning disks and noisy, whirring motors |
| Just like CDs, DVDs store information as a series of coded pits and dots, on the surface of a mirrored disc. Only instead of just sounds or music (audio data), the pits and dots on a DVD can also represent photographs, video clips or entire movies. Just as CD players use lasers to read and decode the audio information on a CD, DVD players use lasers to read and decode DVD video files | HDDs use a tiny electromagnet on the end of a whirring arm to read and write information on a single disk or platter. The platter is usually made of aluminium, covered with a layer of magnetic material and it spins at up to 15,000 revolutions per minute (that's about five times faster than an aeroplane propeller!) as information is transferred back and forth |

## But why do we need DVDs or HDDs, if we can just download stuff straight from the Internet instead?

Because, like I said, everything has to be stored somewhere. Even Internet movies. When you download an Internet movie or video clip, where do you think it comes from?

## Err, I dunno. Someone else's computer?

Right. And how do you think the movie is stored inside that computer?

## Ohhh, I get it. On a hard-disk drive, right?

Right. Or something like it. The Internet is a combination of information storage devices (like computers and servers) and delivery vehicles (like phone lines, broadband links, Wi-Fi transmitters). You can think of the Internet as a huge, global shipping company, with warehouses full of information all over the world, and a fleet of ships, planes and lorries to carry the cargo (information) between them at the speed of light. Without the vehicles, the information couldn't *get about*. But without the storage garages (like HDDs) there would be nowhere to *keep it*.

## So CDs and DVDs were the cargo containers before, and people moved them around. But now the Internet does both?

Right. CDs and DVDs were the last in a long line of data-delivery containers that came before the Internet was powerful enough to store and shuttle information for itself. And, just as Internet music downloads have all but vanquished CDs, Internet video downloads will soon spell the end for the DVDs, too.

## They will?

Yep. Almost certainly. Look at this way . . .

A few hundred years ago, the only way to enjoy music was to go to a live concert.

Clever types like **Thomas Edison** invented sound recording, and soon you could listen to music using 'music storage' devices like . . .

. . . vinyl records, cassette tapes . . .

**Olden days**

Just fifty years ago, your only option for watching movies was to go to a 'live screening' at a cinema.

Then video cassettes were invented.

So I s'pose I should just recycle all my DVDs, then? Not much point in keeping them now . . .

Well, you might want to keep your rare ones and favourites, just as backups (just in case they get erased from the iTunes library or something). Plus you might enjoy looking back at them one day, remembering what it was like 'back in the old days'.

## Like what my grandad does when he breaks out his suitcase of old, blurry photographs?

Exactly. Imagine – one day you could be boring your own grandkids with *Avatar* or *Harry Potter* on DVD . . .

. . . and CDs. Then along came the Internet, and with it online music libraries like . . .

. . . Napster, iTunes and Rhapsody.

From 2004 onwards, music downloads began outselling CD sales every year!

**Now**

By the mid 1980s, millions of people were taking movies home in their boxy, plastic 'video storage' vehicles.

After video cassettes came DVDs (and, since then, HD discs and Blu-Ray discs).

Now movies can be downloaded or streamed over the Internet, fewer and fewer people are buying DVDs each year.

# Music and Movies Crossword

**Across**

1. Buzz _____ astronaut star of 8 across (9).
4. Device that can hold over 10,000 electronic books (1,6).
7. What the 'H' in 'HDD' stands for (4).
8. Animated film about a group of talking toys (3,5).
9. 3D movie about a planet inhabited by blue-skinned aliens called the Na'vii (6).
11. American engineer who invented the first music recording device (6).
12. Cowboy star of 8 across (5).

**Down**

2. Book and movie series about a powerful boy-wizard (5,6).
3. What the 'C' in 'CD' stands for (7).
5. Vinyl disc used to record and play music (6).
6. Type of invisible light used in TV remote controllers (8).
10. What the 'D' in 'DVD' stands for (5).

(Answers on page 134.)

# E-WORLDS AND INTERWEBZ

## Who built the Internet?

No one person or country built the Internet. It began with an experimental computer network designed by the American military. But the World Wide Web we use today was built over three decades, by millions of people, in countries all over the world.

## What? The Internet was a military experiment?

Sort of, yes. In 1969, the United States military's Advanced Research Projects Agency (or ARPA) designed a network of computers that spanned three

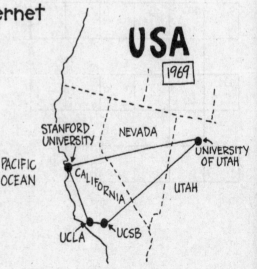

American states (California, Nevada and Utah) and covered a distance of over 2,000 miles. They called it ARPANET. It wasn't the Internet, but it was an internet.

## What do you mean by that?

Well, ARPANET was the first practical, long-distance, **Inter-**communicating **Net**work of computers. And while it isn't the same network we use today (ARPANET was shut down in 1990, by which time today's Internet had grown to replace it), it was perhaps the first working 'internet' the world had ever seen.

*That's how today's Internet eventually got its name: 'Inter-Network' became 'Inter-Net' ... geddit?*

## So what did they build it for? Was it so generals could email orders to soldiers all across the world, like, really quickly?

Errr, no. It wouldn't have been much use for that. When it was first built, ARPANET only linked together four places in the western United States. These four places were all sites of American universities with high-tech electronics laboratories. ARPANET was designed as an experiment – to see if it was possible to send, receive and store information across an interconnected network of computers. The idea was to share information between

**61**

'nodes' (or clusters of computers) located hundreds of miles away from each other.
That way, research information could be easily shared across long distances, and would be kept safe even if one or more computers were stolen or destroyed.

*Or later on 'hacked' by nasty (but clever) computer spies or 'hackers'.

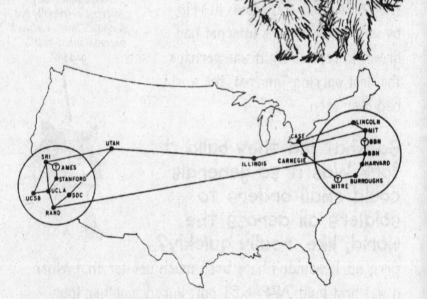

## So did it work?

Yep. The ARPANET experiment was a huge success, and by 1975, it included sixty more 'nodes', in cities spread right across the United States. Then in 1977 programmers in the US and UK managed to link up three separate computer networks in San Francisco, Virginia and London. This showed that an international (even intercontinental) internet was possible, and it kicked off the development of other 'mini-internets' right across the globe. In the 1980s, internets sprang up in Europe (CERNET), Australia (AARNET) and Japan (JUNET). By the end of the decade, these had been linked up with a growing American network (not ARPANET, but a new, non-military network designed to replace it) to form a truly global network.

## So then it got all linked up, and they renamed it the World Wide Web?

Not quite. That name came about kind of by accident. In 1991, British engineer and programmer Tim Berners-Lee invented the first internet browsing program, which eventually allowed every computer on the internet to 'see' every other. He called his program 'WorldWideWeb', but since this was the only way to see the Internet in the 1990s, people started using the phrase 'World Wide Web' to describe the Internet itself. Today, this name still survives in the 'www . . .' that starts every web address (or URL).

Today, there are lots of browser programs, including Microsoft Internet Explorer, Mozilla Firefox, Google Chrome and more. But back then WorldWideWeb was pretty much it.

## Crazy. I always wondered where all those Ws came from.

Well, now you know.

## So what actually is the Internet? I mean, where does it live, and what is it made of?

The Internet now lives all over the world, spread out between millions of 'nodes' worldwide. It's basically made of three things:

**1) Information** – this includes words, numbers, images, sounds, music, video clips, web pages and raw computer data or code.

**2) Information hosts** – these include desktops, laptops, tablets, smartphones, memory drives, computer servers and anything else hooked up to the Internet that can be used to store information.

**3) The global telecommunications network** – including modems, routers, telephone lines, fibre-optic cables, satellites, microwave transmitters and more. Basically, everything that's used to shift information between information hosts.

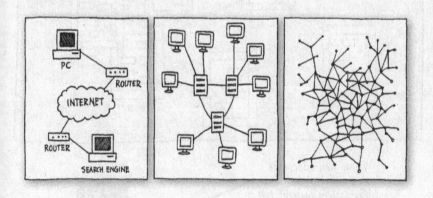

That little lot – all connected together to the brains and fingers of Internet users worldwide – is what makes today's Internet the vast, powerful virtual information monster it is today.

# http://

HTTP stands for hyper-text transfer protocol – it's the Internet's main **networking protocol**. In other words, it's a way for computers in a **network** to **request information** from one another, and to **respond** by sending back the information requested. Basically, http is what keeps all the documents, pictures and pages of the Web linked together. And it's how Web information gets transferred (or routed) between those who **have** it, and those who **want** it.

## HYPERTEXT LINKS

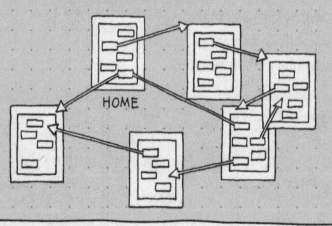

HOME

Some web addresses start with 'ftp', 'smtp' or other letters instead, but 'http' is the most common address starter.

## Whoa. Sounds pretty big.

It is. In fact, it's hard to fathom just how big it has become.

## Go on, then – how big?

That all depends how you measure it. In terms of people or users, the Internet now includes around **1.8 billion** people worldwide. That's roughly a **quarter** of the population of the entire world. In terms of information, the Internet now contains over 5 million terabytes of computer data. To give you an idea of how much that is, the first iPods could store 5 gigabytes' worth of music, which – if you owned one – gave you 'over 1,000 songs in your pocket'. That's around a billionth the amount of data that currently makes up the World Wide Web. In other words, if the Internet were an iPod, you could store over a **trillion** tunes on it. Which is at least twice the total number of stars in our galaxy.

*Although these users aren't spread out very evenly. In the UK and USA for example, roughly two-thirds of the population are on the Internet – 40 million people in the UK, and 220 million in the USA. But in Africa, South America and South-east Asia, less than a tenth of the population is similarly 'hooked up'.*

# Whoa . . .

What's more, that information is shared across over **150 million** websites (and over a **trillion** individual web pages) worldwide.

## Seriously? A trillion web pages? So how long would it take to read them all?

If you read one per minute – without ever stopping to eat, sleep or go to the toilet – it would take round about **31,000 years**. Coincidentally, this is roughly also the age of the entire *Homo sapiens* species. So if you printed out every page on the Internet, crammed it into a time machine and travelled back to give it to the first ever human . . . then his descendants would still be trying to finish it now.

## Actually, I think it'd take a bit longer than that.

Why's that?

## Well, for starters, cavemen couldn't actually read, right?

Ah. Good point.

# Internet Wordsearch

(Answers on page 135.)

```
H G P X R K Q K V S B N U K B Z K A K
B R O W S E R H O F A E W P J S T J W
P I I O L A T E E P B O W W N Q U H X
A Q X I G D Q U S I S B O S E S C U Z
X P N P I L R A O Q A R I N E D O N A
Z K M M Z T E O Z R L T I R L R O Y O
E W E B S I T E R D X Q V I Q W N N T
A E R Q F W H G W E R E J N O E U S S
R B B C V X F I T Q R I L G T W W W O
P P W T L B D R K V P X N W G W A G H
A A Y J F E E T C Q Y Y O U T U B E T
N G U U W P V I N F O R M A T I O N T
E E Y E Y S Y V D E K S R M H R F R P
T D B H G O P C Y K O O B E C A F U O
```

| | | |
|---|---|---|
| ARPANET | browser | Facebook |
| Google | host | HTTP |
| hyper-text | information | link |
| network | node | router |
| server | webpage | website |
| WorldWideWeb | WWW | YouTube |

69

## How does Google search the web so quickly?

It doesn't. Computer programs like Google, Yahoo! And Bing are essential for finding online information. But if they searched the entire Internet for it, you'd still be waiting for an answer years from now. Instead, they look through a kind of 'Internet Index' put together by robots called 'spiders', 'ants' or 'crawlers'.

## You're having me on. That's not right.

What's not right?

## Seriously? I'm supposed to believe that Google is run by an army of robot ants and spiders?

Well, ants and spiders don't actually *run* Google. (Some very, very rich people do that.) But they do *work for* Google. What's more, Google couldn't work *without* them.

# Look, if you don't know the answer to my question, you can just say so . . .

I'm serious! It's true! Of course, they're not real robotic spiders and insects. The Internet is a virtual, electronic library, so it takes virtual, electronic robots to crawl through it and gather information. These so-called 'web crawlers' are actually computer programs, designed for that very purpose.

# But why would you need them at all? I mean, Google is a computer program, right?

Right. Google is an example of a **search engine** – a computer program designed to find information for you on the Web. There are many search engine programs out there, but only a few are used worldwide, and none are used as widely as Google. Other popular search engines include **Yahoo!**, **Bing** and **Ask. com**. But none of these programs actually searches the whole Internet when you type in a word, phrase or question.

# They don't? Why not?

Because, quite simply, there's way too much information out there, and it'd take way too long to do it. Look at it this way – if you had to find out, say, who ruled Egypt during its fourth dynasty, from 2589 to 2566 BC. And you weren't allowed to use the Internet. What would you do?

## I dunno. Go to the library or something. Ask for a book about Egypt.

Okay. Let's say you got there, and the librarian said 'Oh, yes – we've got one of those. It's in here somewhere. Feel free to look around. What then? Would you search through the thousands and thousands of books on the shelves, flicking through each one in turn to see if there's a mention of Egypt or pharaohs? Even if you ignored any books without 'Egypt' in the title, it would still take ages to find the right books, and *even longer* to flick through them for a rare mention of its fourth-dynasty ruler.

## Don't be stupid. Nobody would do it like that.

So what *would* you do?

## I'd ask the librarian where to look.

But how does he or she know where to look?

**They've got an index or something. A big list of which books they have, what they're about and where you can find them. Then you follow those funny numbers on the shelves till you find the right one.**

Exactly! Large libraries use an **index** or **central database** system to keep track of what's on their shelves. Without this, even the best librarian in the world couldn't hope to find the right book (and the right page) among thousands of possible choices. And so it is with the Web.

As you've already learned, the World Wide Web contains over a *trillion* pages of information, and it would take over 31,000 years for a person to read it all. Even the most powerful search program would take at least a year or two to search every word, on every page of the Web, every time you asked it something. So, rather than waste years of your time, search engines

*If you haven't, see 'Who built the Internet?' on page 60 for details.*

such as Google act like virtual librarians. Instead of searching the whole Web for the information you need, they look it up in a huge, central Web database – an index to the library of Internet information.

THE WEB CRAWLER
SCANS BILLIONS OF
WEB PAGES AND
STORES THEM IN...

THE LIBRARY
INDEX. WHERE
THEY WAIT FOR
YOU TO...

CALL THEM UP
ON A COMPUTER.

## So who made the index?

Ahh, you see – *that's* where the robot spiders come in.
Automated 'web crawler' programs (also known as ants,
or spiders) scour the Web day in, day out, reading virtual
labels (called meta-tags) attached to billions of web pages
which tell them what the page (or site) is supposed to
be about. They then compile lists of web page addresses
or (URLs) along with lists of key words that describe
each page. So a web page about the history of Egypt, for
example, might have a list of meta-tags (or keywords) like
this: [Egypt; history; pharaoh; Nile; pyramids; Ramses;
Tutenkhamun . . ] and so on. A web-crawler program
scans (and re-scans, since web information can change
everyday) thousands of web pages this way, and adds the
addresses and keywords it finds to a central database.
*This*, then, becomes the library index that a search engine
like Google will flick through when you type in a word or
search term.

**So that's how search engines get the answers back so fast?**
Right.

**Because the robot ants and spiders have already done all the searching and indexing for them?**
Right. Plus people (usually web-page designers) will add to the index themselves, by *sending* addresses, meta-tags, keywords and other information about their websites to Google and other search engine companies. This helps Google build their database faster, and helps the website owner to get their website found.

**Okay – I think I get it all, now. There's just one more thing that's bothering me . . . Who did rule Egypt from 2589 to 2566 BC?**
Ahh, you'll have to find that out for yourself . . .

Oh, all right then. Turn to page 135.

75

# Game: Speed-Googling!

Search engines like Google are a great way of finding information on the Internet. But sifting through all the results to find the information you really need can be tough work, and is a skill in itself. Grab a friend and test your Googling abilities with this quiz.

Here's how you do it. You need a computer with two browser windows open – one open at www.Google.com, the other at www.e.ggtimer.com. On the e.ggtimer window, type in '5 minutes' into the box to set the countdown. Now grab a piece of paper and a pen, and write the numbers 1-20 down one side. When you're ready to begin, click 'GO!' on the e.ggtimer, flick back to the Google window tab and quickly find as many answers as you can to the questions given opposite before the time runs out. Write the answers down on a piece of paper. For even more fun, try racing a friend! There are two ways to do this: if you have two computers, you can sit side by side, count 3-2-1 and start your e.ggtimers at the same time. If you only have one computer between you, then have one person leave the room (so they don't see the answers the other finds) and go one at a time.

**Ready? Set? *Google!***

1) What is the capital of Kyrgyzstan?
2) On which day does Japan's 'Umi no hi' ('Ocean Day') fall?
3) Name the four US presidents carved into the famous Mount Rushmore.
4) Who was Great Britain's first prime minister?
5) How many of Greece's 6,000 islands are inhabited?
6) What is the atomic number of the element Einsteinium?
7) A female deer is called a doe; what is a female bear called?
8) How tall is the Eiffel Tower?
9) Which ancient Greek author wrote *The Odyssey* and *The Iliad*?
10) In which year did we last see Halley's Comet?
11) When can we expect to see Halley's Comet again?
12) Who built India's famous Taj Mahal?
13) Name the two moons of Mars.
14) Mount Everest is the highest mountain in the world. What is the second highest?
15) What is the official language of the Philippines?
16) Which famous sculptor created *The Thinker*?
17) In terms of land area, what are the world's three largest countries?
18) King Henry VIII had six wives. Which two did he have executed?
19) Which famous composer and violinist wrote *The Four Seasons*?
20) Where do I live?

# Get It Sorted – Snail Mail vs Email

| Snail Mail | Email |
| --- | --- |
| Write your message, shove it in an envelope and write two things on it: 1) the name and address of the person it's going TO, and 2) the name and address of the person it's FROM.* | Write your email using an email program on your computer (like Gmail or Outlook). This message includes the names and electronic addresses of the person it's going TO and also the person it's FROM. |
| Take it to the post office and get it stamped and postmarked with the time (or date) you sent it. This done, it's sorted into a pile based on the general destination, and waits to be sent on its way.** | When you click 'SEND', the email program 'postmarks' the message with the current time and date, and sends it through an Internet connection to an email server (an Internet-linked machine with an email handling program installed). The server then sorts your message into an electronic 'outgoing' pile, which is immediately handed back into the Internet. |

*In the UK, where I grew up, you can get away with leaving this bit out. But in the USA, where I live now, the posties won't take a letter unless you put the sender's name and address on it, too. Since email works more like the American postal system, we'll say you need both things on the envelope for the purposes of our story!*

*\** Either that or you put a stamp on and stick it in a postbox. This adds an extra step, but the end result is the same – your letter gets picked up by a postie, ends up getting sorted at a post office sorting centre somewhere, where it sits in another pile waiting to be picked up again.*

| | |
|---|---|
| A postie transfers your letter to an appropriate vehicle, which drives/sails/flies it to the general area in which the receiver lives. There, it arrives at a local sorting centre and gets sorted into yet another pile based on the local address. | The high-speed Internet now becomes your mail's delivery vehicle, as it speeds through fibre-optic cables and wireless networks to reach an incoming mail server closer to the receiver's real-world address. There, it gets sorted into an incoming mail pile and stored until the receiver is ready to check their email. |
| A local postie picks up his 'local' pile, heads out on his rounds, and drops the letter off at the receiver's address.  | Whenever the receiver gets around to checking their email, they fire up their computer's email program, which contacts the incoming mail server through the Internet, and retrieves the whole store of messages held in the server's electronic P.O. box (or Inbox) |
| Finally, someone at your receiver's address picks up the letter from their postbox (or, possibly, off the doormat) and bingo – your letter has arrived. | Finally, the receiver clicks on the message title, which downloads the message from the server to their computer's Inbox and bingo – email delivered. |
| **Total time taken** – minimum one day, but can take up to a week or more.  | **Total time taken** – half a second, even if the email is being sent from London, UK to Sydney, Australia meaning the email is travelling at 306 million miles per hour, or close to half the speed of light. |

*Email is sent and received in seconds, because the sorting is done at super-speed by computers, and the transporting and delivering is done by moving digital information 'packages' through networked wires and waves at blinding speed.*

# Quick Email Quiz

Test your e-knowledge with this quick multiple-choice quiz. Choose a, b or c for each question, then go to page 135 to see how you did.

**1) Roughly how many emails are sent, worldwide, every day?**
**a)** 1 million
**b)** 10 billion
**c)** 100 billion

**2) How much of this is spam?**
**a)** about 10%
**b)** about 50%
**c)** about 90%

**3) Which country sends the most spam messages per day?**
**a)** India
**b)** USA
**c)** Nigeria

**4) When was the first ever email sent?**
**a)** 1972
**b)** 1982
**c)** 1992

**5) Who was the first head of state to send an email?**
**a)** The president of the United States
**b)** The prime minister of the United Kingdom
**c)** The Queen

# ANDROIDS AND A.I.

## Are some people really robots in disguise?

Sadly, no. At least, not unless you're reading this book some time after the year 2050. Right now, we simply don't have the technology to create humanoid robots (or androids) that look and act 'human' enough to fool us. And although some pretty impressive androids have already been built experts reckon it'll be a long while before truly humanlike robots walk among us, unnoticed.

## So we can build androids, just not ones that can fool us into thinking they're human?

Exactly.

## Why not? I mean, they make those waxwork models of celebrities that look real enough, right? So why not real-looking androids?

Because sculpting a waxwork model is much, much simpler than building a walking, talking android. For a waxwork to look real, it just has to stand there. For an android to look real, it not only has to look like a person, it also has to move, talk and act like a person, too. So far no one has managed to build an android that looks human, walks and moves like a human, and reacts to

OVER 200 MOVABLE JOINTS

OVER 600 SEPARATE MUSCLES

OVER 1,300 POSSIBLE MOVEMENTS (ENGINEERS WOULD SAY WE HAVE OVER 1,300 POSSIBLE DEGREES OF FREEDOM!

NO MORE THAN 100 DEGREES OF FREEDOM !

people and speech in truly realistic, human ways. That's partly because we human beings are hugely complex and sophisticated creatures.

## Smart-bots

If you look up 'clever' in a dictionary, you get something like this:

**Clever** *(adjective)*
1. Nimble or dexterous with the hands or body.
2. Displaying sharp intelligence.
3. Mentally bright, quick or original.
4. Sly or cunning.

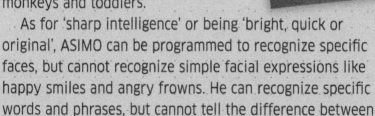

Now by any of those definitions, it's hard to call any modern-day humanoid robots clever.

You may have seen Honda's ASIMO on YouTube walk, climb stairs (and even jog) but he can't leap, roll, crawl, peel a banana or climb a ladder using his hands. That makes him considerably less nimble than most monkeys and toddlers.

As for 'sharp intelligence' or being 'bright, quick or original', ASIMO can be programmed to recognize specific faces, but cannot recognize simple facial expressions like happy smiles and angry frowns. He can recognize specific words and phrases, but cannot tell the difference between a happy giggle and an angry shout. He can be programmed to perform a sequence of dance steps, but will not learn to move for himself by copying the movements of others. In fact, ASIMO can't do anything he isn't specifically programmed to do beforehand. That makes him less intelligent than most pet dogs. And as for 'sly' or 'cunning' – well, let's just say that ASIMO will never try to sneak a sausage off your breakfast plate, or cheat at a game of cards. He just doesn't know how.

For engineers, the 'cleverest' (or most impressive) robots are those that are both nimble (or dexterous) and useful. When asked to name a clever robot, robotics experts will usually point to complex assembly or handling robots used in car manufacturing or heavy industry. The most advanced ones have more freedom of movement than a human arm or hand, and can switch tools by themselves so that at one time a hand is a welder, another a cutter, another a grabber and so on. While it's perhaps no more 'intelligent' than humanoid robots like ASIMO, it can do things human workers can't do, and can practically put together an entire car by itself. It's hard to say that's not clever, by comparison.

# So how good are today's androids, and where can you find them?

Some of them are pretty good (far from perfect, but convincing enough to make you look twice!). The most advanced androids are currently being built in Korea and Japan.

# Like that ASIMO robot?

Not so much him, no. While ASIMO was created to mimic human movements (specifically, walking movements), he wasn't really built to look human. He's a humanoid robot, but he's not really an android. If you covered ASIMO with skin, he still wouldn't look human – he's square-edged, stocky and has no human facial features at all. But other Japanese and Korean androids do look human.

**Osaka University, Japan:** Doll-like female **Actroid** robot revealed at the International Robot Exhibition in Tokyo. The original Actroid had human-like body proportions, hair and facial features, but could not stand up, and could only move its arms and facial 'muscles' in very limited ways.

**Repliee Q1** (new, improved Actroid) unveiled at the 2005 World's Fair in Nagoya. This Actroid had realistic silicon skin, and ten more degrees of freedom (DOF) in its movement than the original model, making its facial features and hand gestures much more realistic.

**2003**

**2005**

**Korean Institute of Industrial Technology:** Education and entertainment, **Eve-R1** unveiled. Like Repliee Q1 – a seated, female android with realistic facial expressions (like fear, surprise and anger) and arm gestures.

**Eve-R2** revealed – a free-standing female android with enhanced facial expressions (including boredom and irritation) which could chat with children in a classroom, or mime along with pre-recorded songs on stage.

**DER-03** (its predecessors were the Dramatic Entertainment Robots DER-01 and DER-02): a free-standing (and attractive-looking) female android, had such realistic features and movements that she fooled (and even frightened) many reporters.

**Japan's National Institute of Advanced Industrial Science: HRP-4C** – a walking, talking, singing, 'girlbot' with a range of realistic human walking movements, dance movements and facial expressions. Her realistic skin, hair and other human-like features only extend to her face, head, neck and hands – the rest of her body is more or less the right shape, but is covered with metal and plastic body-armour that makes her look like a *Star Wars* stormtrooper. But she's probably the most realistic-looking android to date.

## 2008

## 2009

## 2010

The correct term for a female humanlike robot is actually **gynoid**, rather than android. Best remember that for the future, if you don't want to offend your robot girlfriends . . .

**Eve-R3** performed an entire musical stage play alongside human actors, playing the lead role in *Snow White and the Seven Dwarfs*!

**Geminoids** are androids built to look exactly like their masters or creators, and Japanese robotics professor, Hiroshi Ishiguro, has built one modelled on himself (Geminoid HI), on a Japanese model friend (Geminoid F) and Danish Robotics professor Henrik Scharfe (Geminoid DK). While none of these can walk or talk like their masters, they look real enough at first glance to fool many people.

As of 2010, **'Fembots'** – based on the Actroid DER-03 – have been available to buy in Japan. For the tidy sum of 20 million Yen (around £150,000), one of these realistic female androids could be sitting on your sofa – singing songs, giggling at your jokes and more. But don't expect her to cook you dinner, or head out with you to meet your friends. The Fembot cannot move at all from the waist down.

It'll probably be another fifty or sixty years, at least, before we can build androids that can not only look human, but can also understand natural human speech, understand the things they see with their digital eyes and understand human actions, motivations and emotional states.

## Once that happens, could androids start to replace people?

In some ways, yes – they could. There will almost certainly come a time – probably sometime in the latter half of this century – when buying and running a robot will be cheaper than paying a human worker to do the same job, for the same length of time. When that happens, robots will start to pop up everywhere, replacing human workers in the more boring, menial jobs like sitting at roadside toll booths, or giving directions and information at train stations, airports and

*For more about this see 'How many robots are there in the world?' on page 95.*

shopping centres. And, as robots become more advanced, the number of jobs they can do will become greater and greater.

# Get It Sorted – Intelligent Robots

Experts reckon that at the current rate of development, the first truly intelligent robots — nimble, agile robots with true artificial intelligence — will probably arrive within the latter half of this century (i.e. some time after 2050). Already, engineers are making small steps toward this. The **XPERO** robot, built by a group of European universities working together, can learn about its own movement and environment by observing and experimenting, much as human babies and toddlers do. Meanwhile, the child-like **CB2** robot — built by Japanese engineers at Osaka University — not only looks like a human toddler (complete with human-like eyes, eyelids, lips, ears and skin), it learns to interact with people by watching their facial expressions, just as a human baby would.

**But what if they decide to replace us altogether? Like, wage war, start building themselves, disguise themselves as us and take over the world?**

Not likely. For starters, they'll still have human programmers, who will build in safety circuits and programming rules that prevent them from harming people, and force them to obey human commands, no matter what.

**But what if those circuits got busted, or the programming went wrong?**

Well, then we'd have a problem.

**I guess we'd better be nice to our robots. You know – just in case . . .**

# The world's biggest and smallest robots

The smallest robot is so tiny that you could fit a million of them inside a blood cell. The largest is a 12-metre-tall transforming robot dinosaur that breathes fire, crushes cars and eats aeroplanes.

## Microscopic robots:

The world's tiniest robot to date was built by a Chinese university research team in 2009, led by American chemistry professor Nadrian Seeman. They built it using strands of deoxyribonucleic acid (or DNA) – the same stuff found within the cells of all living creatures – folded up like bits of origami paper until they took the desired shape. The result was a two-armed nanobot measuring just 150 nanometres (or millionths of a millimetre) long, and 50 nanometres wide. This 'bot could then be used to place other chemical molecules together and build new sub-microscopic structures. A bit like a crane on a construction site. Only about 50 billion times smaller. As a grand finale, Dr Seeman then went on to create a pair of DNA 'robot legs', which scissor back and forth as if walking.

Engineers in Korea, Japan and elsewhere have built controllable microbots that look like tiny caterpillars. Designed to inch their way through blood vessels and other body tissues, some measure less than 500 micrometres (or half a millimetre) long. They're controlled by two, microscopic actuators that allow them to follow one of two commands ('move forward', or 'turn'), and are powered by tiny electrical currents they absorb from surfaces around them.

## Supersized robots:

The **Fanuc m-2000** and the **Kuka TITAN** are mighty industrial robots. These are both heavy-duty 'handling bots' – huge, robotic arms with powerful claws and grippers. They stand up to 3 metres (10 feet) tall, weigh up to 5,000 kg (5 tonnes) and can lift loads of up to 1,200 kg (1.2 tonnes). One Kuka TITAN 'bot can lift an entire car 3 metres (10 feet) into the air, while a second attaches the wheels. Their grasping claws could crush a person like a crisp packet, so for that reason factory workers are kept completely out of the rooms where these monster robots work, all the time that they are working.

The biggest, scariest robot built to date is probably
**Robosaurus** – a 12-metre (40-foot) tall transforming robot
dinosaur. Robosaurus was built in 1989, by American
inventor (and Transformers fan) Doug Malewicki. 'Robo' as
he calls it, can crush cars and planes with its massive claws
and jaws, and it breathes fire through flamethrowers set
into each nostril. The operator (or pilot) sits in the head
of this metallic beast and controls the claws, jaws and
flamethrowers from there. When not in use, Robosaurus can
transform itself into a box-shaped lorry trailer for towing
around on roads.

# How many robots are there in the world?

It's hard to know for sure, but there are probably over *nine million* working robots on the planet. If you know where to look, you can find them in factories, farms, power plants and mines all over the world. They're even invading our schools and homes! Robots do a huge range of different jobs for us – most of which humans could not (or would rather not) do for themselves. That's why robots are on the rise.

# Nine million? That's a lot of robots! That's, like, an entire city full of them!

That's right, it is. Of course, these nine million robots don't all live in the same place. But if they did, they would fill a huge city like New York or London. Put another way, the world's current robot population is bigger than the human population of Scotland or Sweden, and more than *twice* that of Ireland or Israel. So, if they wanted to, the robots could happily fill a whole *country*.

# Whoa. But what would they call it?

'Robot-o-stan', maybe? 'The Robot Republic'?

# How about 'Robo-nesia'?

Nice!

# Thank you. I try. So what are all those robots up to? I mean, how many jobs can a robot really do?

Robots get up to all *sorts* of things, and they do more jobs than you can possibly imagine. Engineers often classify robots into three main types or groups: **industrial robots, professional robots** and **personal (or service) robots**. Industrial and professional robots come in a wide range of different shapes and sizes. They typically do jobs that are considered too **dull**, **dirty** or **dangerous** for human workers. Robot engineers call these sorts of tasks 'the three Ds'. And believe me, there are a lot of them.

# What about the other ones? What did you call 'em – the **personal** robots?

Yep – they're on the rise, too. Personal service robots include everything from robot vacuum cleaners and

96

lawnmowers to robot toys, pets, learning 'bots and hobby 'bots. Almost a million **Roombas** (a popular robot vacuum cleaner) were sold in 2008 alone, and with floor sweeping and

mopping versions joining the party, soon millions of homes could have robot cleaners trundling around their floors. In the last decade, toy robots like Pleo, RoboRaptor and RoboSapien have become playpals for thousands of kids around the world, and the new generation of toy robots and pets – with advanced AI and speech recognition – will leave those early efforts in the dust. Meanwhile, Japan and South Korea are working feverishly on educational 'learning 'bots' for schools, and thousands of robot hobbyists (or 'makers') are currently designing, building and battling their own DIY robots. These are often built at home with parts purchased from the Internet, or printed from free online blueprints using 3D printers.

Check out the 'Robo-Pet Shop' on page 102 for more about robot pets.

# 'It's a dirty job, but someone's got to do it'

Match the job descriptions opposite to the **Dull**, **Dirty** or **Dangerous** columns – you might find that some of them appear in more than one column.

It's not that humans can't do most of the dull jobs. But it is impossibly boring to do the same tasks hour after hour, day after day, year in, year out. Humans can only work so fast, and so hard, before they drop. And they can't work too long without stopping to rest, eat, drink, pee, sleep and go home to see their families.

Many work environments – like mines, forges, oil rigs and nuclear reactors – are dangerous enough to claim thousands of human lives in industrial accidents every year. As robots become more flexible, mobile and agile, more and more of the truly dirty jobs are being handed over to our metallic friends.

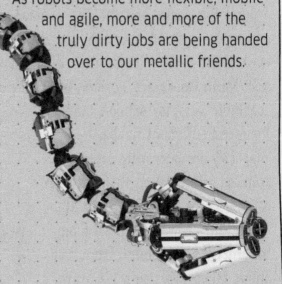

Defuse bombs*

Salvage shipwrecks

Milk cows

Perform brain surgery

Pack products into boxes

Assembling gadgets

Repair legs of an oil-rig platform

Dig and drill in coal mines

Fill milk cartons on a conveyor belt

Heavy lifting in car assembly plants

Lifting and lowering fuel rods in the heart of a nuclear reactor

Unblock clogged sewage pipes

| Dull | Dirty | Dangerous |
|------|-------|-----------|
|      |       |           |
|      |       |           |
|      |       |           |
|      |       |           |
|      |       | * For more on these, see 'Will future battles be fought by robots?' on page 126. |

99

## Wow. It sounds like **everyone** will own a robot before long. So will they?

Probably not *everyone*, no. As popular as robots are becoming, getting people to *buy* robots depends on how cheaply we can build them, and how wealthy each household is. Right now, the cost of batteries and motors is holding robot development back as it makes home robots too expensive for most people to build or buy.

**Boo.**

Even so, around 2 million more robots are being built and sold each year. So at the current rate there will be almost a **billion** robots on the planet by 2050, and almost **2 billion** by the end of the century. That's nearly a third of the human population of the world! And who knows – once new power sources and technologies become available, there could be far more.

## Like, the robots could outnumber the people?

Yup. Could be.

## That's a little scary.

Let's just hope they keep doing
what they're told. Otherwise you'll be
fighting off Roombas and RoboRaptors
all day long . . .

# 'Robo-Pet Shop – for all your robot animal needs'

### Woof-woof!

Your own playful puppy – without the mess – **AIBO** by Sony can walk and play and perform – he can 'sit', 'stay' and 'roll over' (or even 'dance', 'handstand' and 'somersault'!). Puppy AIBO learns your commands. Limited availability – no longer in production. Yours for only £2,000!

## The purr-fect companion!

Want a cuddly moggy, but allergic to cat hair? Then you need **Yu-me Neko** ('Dream Cat') by Sega. Covered with soft artificial fur Yu-me Neko purrs softly when stroked, miaows for attention and rolls on its back for a belly rub. Just don't tug its tail or it will yowl and hiss at you!

## Pets are good for you!

Medical studies have revealed that pet owners often recover from illness more quickly than people without pets, as having a loving cat or dog around can help reduce stress, and keep your spirits up. Unfortunately, real animals aren't allowed on most hospital wards, as they have to be kept very clean to prevent the spread of bacteria. But with a robo-pet even the very ill can enjoy having a faithful or fuzzy pal, and get many of the benefits of keeping a real animal.

## Rooooaaaarrrrr!

It's the new age of the dinosaurs! Now available, your very own robotic baby dinosaur, **Pleo**. Complete with complex microprocessor and over 38 sensors to detect light, motion, touch and sound, Pleo is an ideal companion. Take your Pleo to meet another and they will recognize and talk to each other – but take care because they can also catch colds from each other.

# Get your robo-animal working for you

### Ssssssneaky sssssnake-bot

Exclusive! Still in testing! Suitable for search and rescue operations – the Omnitread Serpentine is a 1.2-metre (4-foot) robotic snake that can crawl over any type of terrain, slither into holes just 10 cm (4 inches) wide and tunnel beneath heavy bricks or boulders to find people trapped beneath.

### Spy-bots!

Now available! Robo-roaches that can scuttle into pitch-black rooms, feel their way around walls and obstacles with robotic antennae and take infrared or thermal pictures with on-board cameras. At the moment these are too big and slow to be of much use.

2-metre (6-foot), camouflaged robot snake equipped with a digital camera – wriggles through undergrowth to sneak up and spy on enemy positions. These are still being tested by the Israeli army.

## Coming soon!

Robot bees and robot beetles – will fly unseen into secret areas, snapping pictures and gathering information.

For more on these, see 'Will future battles be fought by robots?' on page 126.

## Cyborg Bugs!

The ultimate spy accessory – a team of researchers has successfully attached computer chips, cameras and electrodes, to real beetles, creating freaky 'cyborg bugs' that can be steered towards targets by human controllers. By sending signals from a computer chip stuck to the beetle's back to wires embedded in the beetle's brain and wing muscles, engineers steered a beetle through an obstacle course with several left and right turns, and got it to stop and land. The future is here.

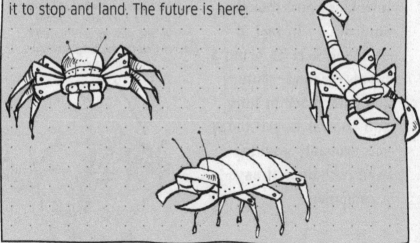

# INTO THE FUTURE

## What will computers be like in a hundred years' time?

Computers are developing so rapidly that it's difficult – even for experts – to imagine what a twenty-second-century computer will look like. They will certainly be more complex, more powerful and more a part of our everyday lives. They might be built with proteins, with bits of DNA or with tiny packets of light. And the quaint old keyboard-and-mouse one day may be replaced with brain interfaces and thought control . . . In fact, if someone were to bring a twenty-second-century computer back in time and show it to you today, you probably wouldn't even recognize it as a computer.

*This is not, by the way, likely to happen. Time-travel – at least into the past – is almost certainly impossible. Otherwise, someone would have already done it. Think about **that** for too long, and your head will explode.*

# Why not?

Well, for starters, they probably won't be built with the same types of electronic chips and circuits you'd find inside a computer today. The speedy development of computers has been based on the ability to make smaller and smaller components and circuits – from the mechanical valves and switches of the early computers to the digital electromagnetic switches on a modern microprocessor chip. But we're now approaching the limit for how small we can make our microchips. Today's microchips are built (mostly) with layers of silicon, and

NOBODY MOVE, I'VE DROPPED MY CHIP!!

you can only slice layers of silicon so thinly before they fall apart. So, if engineers are to cram any more components on to their chips (and continue to double computer processing power every couple of years), then they'll have to find another way of building them. Thankfully, computer scientists across the globe are already working on alternative types of processors that could be made far smaller (and therefore far more powerful) than those built with silicon chips.

# Future Processors

## Nanocomputers

Using nanomaterials such as carbon nanotubes (less than a thousand times thinner than a human hair), engineers are building computer components just 2-3 nanometres wide – more than ten times smaller than those found on today's microchips – creating the world's first nanocomputers.

## Light speed

Engineers are attempting to make transistors using individual packets of light (or photons), creating superfast photon computers.

## Biocomputers

Some engineers are experimenting with bacteria and biological molecules, building organic biocomputers by growing bits of protein or DNA on fatty membranes, much like the ones that surround the cells in your body. If that works, then computers might end up looking more like fleshy lungs and livers than boxy, plastic gadgets.

In future computers, input devices like the keyboard, mouse and touch-screen may well be replaced with voice recognition modules, or even mind-reading brain-computer interfaces (or BCIs) that allow you to type and browse the Internet with your thoughts alone.

## You mean control a computer just with your brain? Like telepathy?

Something like that, yes.

## Is that even possible?

Not only is it possible, it has already been done. EEGs (or Electro-encephalograms) have been used by scientists and doctors for decades, in order to monitor electrical patterns (i.e. brainwaves) in patients and test subjects. You've probably seen them on TV.

Basically, a bundle of sensor wires (or a cap covered with them) is placed on the patient's head. These measure electricity conducted through the skull and display the brainwaves on a computer monitor. By attaching those sensors to different types of devices, you can do more than just display your brainwaves – you can use them to *control* things.

A few years back, engineers unveiled the first thought-controlled computer cursor, or 'telepathic mouse', which allowed people with full-body paralysis to move an onscreen cursor up, down, left and right. Now, computer software company G-Tec have released the first thought-controlled **typing** interface, called **Intendix**. This works by displaying a screenful of keyboard characters (letters, numbers, space bar and so on), and lighting each one up, in turn, with a series of quick flashes. The user wears a brainwave-measuring EEG cap, and stares at the letter they want. When they see their chosen letter light up, it causes a brief 'jump' in their brainwaves. This is picked up by the EEG, relayed to a word processing or email program and used to type that letter in a document or message.

## That's just crazy.

It's crazy, but it works. With practice, users can type at a rate of one letter per second. This is still very slow compared with regular keyboard typing or speech. And for now, it's only really useful for disabled people who cannot move, speak or communicate in other ways. But, in time, this technology will likely develop to the point where you can 'type' whole words, sentences and messages in seconds, with your thought alone. Soon, you'll be pinging friends and updating your webpage just by thinking about it . . .

## That sounds almost like magic!

Well, as the great science-fiction writer Arthur C. Clarke once said, 'Any sufficiently advanced technology is indistinguishable from magic.' With enough time to develop, computer technology could make 'magical' things like mind control and thought-messaging a part of our everyday future lives.

## It also sounds a bit scary. You wouldn't want everything you thought about turning up online, would you?

Nahhh, I'm sure it'd be fine . . .

[Oh, look, there's Dave! Hey, Dave!]

[Howzitgoin'?]

[Not bad. I haven't changed my underpants in three days.]

[Wait – what?]

[Oops.]

[LOL]

# What will future phones be like?

Home telephones (or 'land-lines') are already becoming a thing of the past — replaced by computers or home entertainment systems that make video calls. As for smartphones, they will continue to shrink and develop new uses. One day soon, we could be 'wearing' these mini-computers invisibly in our clothing, and viewing the world through their digital eyes.

# Wow. So in the future there will be no phones?

Probably not. At least not as we know them today. Already, more and more people worldwide are using online calling systems like **Skype** and **FaceTime**, which let you place calls from a desktop, laptop or tablet. This is usually far cheaper than placing an old-school phone call – especially over long distances – and if webcams are available, you can make video calls to four or five people at once.

In most places, you can also make video calls through an Internet-linked digital TV or games console. The newest

Xbox and PlayStation consoles already combine most of the functions of a home computer, television, games console, and digital media player, all controlled from the same screen. For people with these, there is no need for a separate telephone, stereo, satellite TV receiver, and Blu-Ray player. So basically home telephone sets are *history*.

## Will most smartphones become video-phones, too?

That's hard to say. Though most smartphones *already* contain video-calling technology, people don't seem to use mobile video-calling that much. Possibly because holding the phone out in front of yourself in the 'selfie' position is awkward and uncomfortable for any length of time. Others just don't *like* being seen while they talk, or just prefer to text. So audio calls and text messaging may hang on for a while yet.

But then there's *far* more in store for the smartphones than just turning them into portable video-phones . . .

## Like what?

Many communication experts reckon that within a few decades, mobiles will shrink, disappear and turn into 'invisible computers' that help us manage our entire lives.

But how can they get any **smaller**? I mean, seriously – you can hardly hold on to the ones we have now. My dad can't see the screen on his without his glasses, and I'm always losing mine. My phone, that is. Not my glasses. Although I do lose those a lot, too . . .

That's true – mobile phones recently reached a point where they can't *get* much smaller, as the input devices (such as keypad buttons and touchscreens) and output devices (such as screen displays and speakers) become too awkward to use if they're made any smaller. (In fact, the latest smartphones have rebounded, and are *bigger* than those that came before!) But what if you had a flexible keypad on the sleeve of your jacket, or a digital screen display projected on the inside of your sunglasses?

## That would be **awesome**. Could that really work?

They're already here. Google have made the **Google Glass** wearable smartphone/computer, which projects 'augmented reality' images before one eye, adorning everything you see with computerized links and labels. Through this, wearers can 'see' shop prices and restaurant menus, browse their websites, even recognize other Google Glass wearers at a distance! Although these have yet to catch on with everyone, chances are, there's more of this kind of thing to come . . .

# Eyephones – no, really!

Some engineers are working on eyephones – visual displays that are projected on to contact lenses, or even directly on to the retinas of your eyeballs! In theory, display shades and eyephones could overlay images and information on to the real world as you look at it. So you could follow virtual arrows to a Google-mapped destination, or look into shop windows and see the prices hovering above all the items. This is known as augmented reality (or AR), and many experts believe systems like this will become a part of everyday life in the near future.

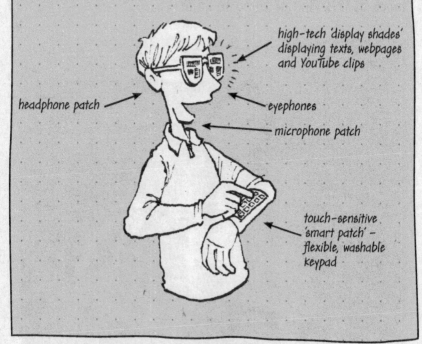

high-tech 'display shades' displaying texts, webpages and YouTube clips

headphone patch

eyephones

microphone patch

touch-sensitive 'smart patch' – flexible, washable keypad

# What will future videogames be like?

Future videogames will be spectacular to look at, mirroring real-life scenes in eye-popping 3D. So realistic, in fact, that it'll be hard to tell whether you're watching someone play a game, or watching a *real* race, battle or sporting event on TV. There will also be many more types of games, more people playing together online, and more people playing games in general. Some gamers may even spend most of their time living and working in a virtual, global 'gameworld'.

## G-g-g-g- . . . what? . . . that's . . . can I . . . uhhhhh . . .

Eh? What's the matter?

## There's so much **brilliance** and **coolness** going on in what you just said that I don't know where to begin . . .

Okay. Just take a breath. Relax.

## Whew! Okay. I'm fine now. So what will the actual games be like?

The latest video console games are already incredible to look at, and unbelievably realistic to play. As the power and graphics of computers and consoles continue to improve, they'll get even better. Driving games will have cars racing on tracks and city streets rendered in amazing, real-life detail, perhaps merging with mapping systems like Google Maps to show actual buildings, landmarks and cars flashing by, in real time! Flight simulators will depict aeroplanes and airports in super-realistic detail, and players will fly through rain and snowstorms updated in real-time by online weather services. If it's raining outside, it'll be raining in your game.

## Will they be 3D, too?

The move to 3D gaming has already begun, and as 3D screen technology improves, it'll start to appear in almost every game available. As game control interfaces get better, old-school game controllers will probably start to disappear, too. Already movement-sensing motion controllers – like the PlayStation Move and Xbox Kinect – are popular with gamers worldwide. Eventually, devices like this will probably take over completely, and almost all games will be controlled with natural, whole-body movements. Whether you're

driving, shooting or fighting off ninjas with your awesome kung-fu skills, it'll be done with minimal props (maybe a pair of gloves and a frisbee-like steering wheel) and a lot of moving your hands and feet through empty space.

## Get It Sorted — 3D in the Future

There are lots of different ways of creating a 3D effect. But all of them rely on **stereoscopic vision**, and fooling the brain into thinking **two separate 2D images** are actually **one single 3D image**. Instead of wearing clunky glasses with red and green lenses (see the activity below to make your own 3D glasses) which give you headaches, in the future we'll be watching 3D films and playing 3D videogames on **Parallax Barrier 3DTVs**, where all the 3D-creating

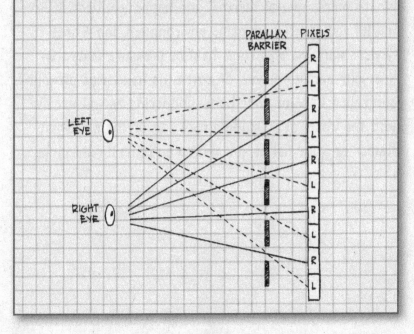

trickery occurs on the screen, and there's no need to wear glasses at all. Instead, a gridlike screen in front of the main TV screen (called a **parallax barrier**) flips between two different shapes, allowing light through at different angles at different times. This ensures only one set of images reaches each eye, which creates a 3D image effect in the brain. Some 3DTVs have permanent parallax screens (so 3D is always on'), while others have LCD parallax screens that can be switched off. This makes the flickering parallax barrier transparent, and returns the TV to ordinary 2D. The effect still isn't perfect. But because we can see these 3D screens without special glasses we can now put them on anything with a screen.

## Sweeeeeet.

What's more, special thermal and haptic feedback devices will let you touch your game environment, too. These devices work via electronic heat or pressure pads that line your gaming gloves, or cover the handgrips on your controller. Imagine your hands juddering as you wrestle with the wheel of a skidding race car, or the satisfying thwack on your fist as you thump an unfortunate ninja.

## Too cool!

Some games may even feature whole haptic bodysuits that – when combined with 3D displays or eyephones – will create seamless virtual reality (VR) worlds that you can not only **see** and **hear**, but also **touch** and **feel**.

*For more about eyephones, see 'What will future phones be like?' on page 112.*

---

# Activity: make your own 3D glasses!

Want to create your own 3D images and view them in the comfort of your own home? Follow these simple steps, and let the 3D eye-boggling begin.

**1)** Go to a local joke or toy shop, and buy a pair of plastic glasses with frames but no lenses. Alternatively, you can ask a family member if they have an old pair of sunglasses they want to get rid of, and carefully press the lenses out. Or you can make your own out of cardboard (measure your face and the distance between your eyes first, so that they fit properly).

**2)** Now find an art shop, and ask for two small sheets of coloured, semi-transparent acetate plastic – one red, and one blue.

**121**

**3)** At home, place the glasses on the red acetate paper, draw round the left eyepiece, cut out the shape you just drew, stick it to the glasses (making a coloured left lens) using sellotape. Now place the glasses on the blue paper, draw round the right eyepiece, and repeat for the right side. You should now have a pair of 3D glasses with a red left lens and a blue right lens.

**4)** Now go to http://www.3d-image.net/gallery.php, and use your glasses to view the 3D images on the page. You can also download free 3D-imagemaking software from this page, and make your own 3D pictures. Enjoy!

## This just gets better and better! So you'll be right **inside** the game, and it'll look just like real life?

Well, maybe not exactly like real life. Creating complete, photo-realistic VR worlds would take more computing power than most consoles are likely to have for a long, long time. But the goal of VR isn't to recreate the real world perfectly – it's just to make the game feel *real enough* to fool your brain. With the right gear, you can do that without photo-perfect graphics. VR and natural motion controllers also allow **more different types** of games to be created, and more **uses** to be found for games besides just 'play'.

## Like what?

Like training games that teach you how to ride a motorbike, sail a yacht, fix a car engine or build a house. Trainee doctors can learn how to do operations with virtual scalpels and organs. Trainee policemen could learn how to search for clues in virtual crime scenes.

The list is almost endless. One day, games like this will probably become a part of school lessons and college courses. Imagine if your homework tonight was 'play virtual surgeon and complete level 3: heart transplant'.

## You mean play games for homework? Now you're talking.

It could happen, and *soon*. In the future, people won't just be playing with videogames, many will also be *working* with them. In online, Internet-linked games like *World of Warcraft*, players already form groups, work together, design outfits, buildings and furniture, and trade clothing and other items for real money. In the future, videogames will merge with social networking systems like Facebook to create **virtual workplaces and businesses**. Virtual 'game-worlds' will contain real shops and services, with real people working in them all day long. Virtual game characters from opposite sides of the globe will meet, talk and trade real-world goods and services in Internet gameworld locations. And they'll get paid to do it.

## Ha! I **knew** it! My mum's always telling me to lay off the videogames cos they're a waste of time. But if I'll be playing games for a living then what's the point in homework and school?

Well, if you want to actually *get* that videogame job, you'll still have to do your schoolwork so you can learn about how computers and businesses work, and how to work in teams with other people (whether they're in the real world or virtual world). For that, you'll need to know your maths, science and English. And if you work with virtual team-mates from across the world, you'll still need to learn their languages, their cultures and the countries they come from. So you'll need foreign languages, geography and world history, too. And if you don't want to turn into a pale, wheezing blob sitting in front of a computer screen, you'll still need to get outside and play real sports and games to stay healthy.

## (Sigh.) Okaaaay. A bit of homework, some footy outside and then it's back to some serious gaming, okay? After all, it's for my **future**, right?

Better ask your mum – that one's not up to me!

# Will future battles be fought by robots?

Yes, they will. In fact, robot drones are *already* helping to fight battles in several war-torn regions of the world. Like it or not, robots are already part of many modern armies, navies and air forces. And by the look of it, the world's robot fighting forces will only get bigger in the future.

# Seriously?! Robots are actually out fighting wars, right now? Where?

Right now, there are robot drones on patrols and missions in various parts of the Middle East and Asia. Most of these are owned and operated by the United States, the United Kingdom or Israel. But word has it that over forty countries across the globe are either operating or building their own military robots, too.

# In the air

The most common military robots are **unmanned aerial vehicles** (or **UAVs**), which fly airborne, scouting, spying or attack missions, although, technically, it's the human controllers or pilots (who are often thousands of miles away) who are doing the spying, shooting and bombing – the robot drone is just the tool or weapon that allows them to do it.

- The **RQ-11 Raven** drone, for example, measures just 130 cm (55 inches) across, and weighs less than 2 kg (4 lb). But it can fly over 10 km (6 miles) on a single scouting mission, at speeds of up to 60 mph (100 kph). Ravens are mostly used to take pictures of enemy camps and targets, using their on-board digital or infrared cameras.
- The **MQ-8 Fire Scout** looks like a fullsize helicopter, only with no see-through cockpit or windows.
- The fearsome **MQ-9 Predator** combat drone is a full-size aeroplane with a 20-metre (66-foot) wingspan, weighing over 2 tonnes (5,000 lb) even before it's loaded with laser-guided bombs and missiles.

# On the ground

## Unmanned ground vehicles (UGVs)

- Bomb-disposal robots have been used for decades in war zones to remove landmines, car-bombs and other explosive booby-traps.

- Miniature tank-bots roll into houses looking for lurking enemies.

- Oversized beetle-bots can scuttle up walls and peer into windows with their camera-laden antennae.

- The Boston Dynamic **'Big Dog'** behaves literally like a helpful dog. It has four dog-like legs that allow it to walk, trot and leap over obstacles that would be tricky for wheels or tank-tracks to roll over.

US Army engineers are already imagining a future combat system (or FCS) for their troops, in which each soldier is accompanied by a whole pack of up to twelve helpful 'bots – ranging from hovering robot scouts and spotters to trundling or trotting robot 'packbots' (like the Big Dog) laden with gear.

# Why are fighting robots so popular?

Well, as we've already said, robots are handy for the 'three Ds' – things so dull, dirty or dangerous that no human really wants to do them. And one thing's for certain: while war may not be dull, it's certainly a dirty, dangerous business. From an army commander's point of view, robots are pretty marvellous. For starters, there's no need to recruit or train robot soldiers – you just build them, and they're yours. And once you have your robot troops there's no need to pay them, feed them, or keep them happy. A robot never gets hungry, never gets stressed or depressed. And it will work or fight for years without rest, through freezing winter nights or endless days in the blazing desert sun. Perhaps best of all, no one really cares when a robot is damaged or destroyed. It's either rebuilt, or forgotten about. But there are no hospital bills to pay, no funerals to attend and no human families left behind to mourn the loss. Looked at this way, you could argue that replacing human troops with robots saves lives – as fewer human soldiers, sailors and pilots are put at risk.

**But isn't battling with robots a bit – you know – risky? I mean, what if one of them made a mistake and bombed the wrong house? Or went crazy and shot an innocent person?**

Well, some people would argue that this happens to *human* pilots and soldiers, too. In fact, according to the latest research, robots have been found to be *more reliable* than people, as they have no fear or anger, and are less likely to make mistakes in the heat of battle.

That said, combat robots (or drones) are also built with special 'failsafe' mechanisms, so that they can't fire upon targets without a human giving the command (or 'pulling the trigger'). So as long as humans are always in control, making the final life–or–death decisions, then we shouldn't have to worry about rogue 'Terminators' flipping out and shooting people all by themselves.

Of course, some people have pointed out that getting robots to do our dirty work makes it more likely that we'll wage wars, resulting in more deaths, not less. After all, if you're thousands of miles away from where the battle is raging – shooting and bombing via remote control – then waging war could feel more like a videogame than the real thing. Only it's not a game, because real people are getting hurt.

## But what if it was all just robots-versus-robots? What if robot armies just fought our battles for us, with no human soldiers or victims involved?

Good question. You could say that this would be the best kind of battle, since no human lives need be lost. But if you think about it, eventually, one side would lose (i.e. run out of working robots) and start to advance. Then it wouldn't be long before they encountered real people, and it was robots-versus people once more. Now instead of facing an army of living, breathing human soldiers, the 'losers' would be facing a horde of battle-hardened robots, all trundling, buzzing and swarming their way into town. I wouldn't want to face that, would you?

## I'd rather not face either, thank you very much. Can't we just avoid wars altogether, and find a way to get along instead?

Well, that's not up to the robots – that's up to us . . .

# ANSWERS

## Page 13: Computer Bits and Pieces

| Part | Job |
| --- | --- |
| Keyboard | used to input characters and program the computer |
| Monitor | displays text, images and video onscreen |
| Mouse | controls cursor, selects icons and scrolls text |
| Motherboard | creates a base for most of the computer's essential parts |
| RAM | the computer's temporary memory bank |
| Hard-disk drive | The computer's permanent memory bank |
| CPU | the computer's core or central processing unit |

## Page 23: Geekspeak

1(a). 2(c). 3(b). 4(a). 5(c).

```
T U K M U U O F V M R R C H A R L I E T
K U A X Z U L U D I T S E E G A L Q N O
E M B Z D N O X V Z M G B I I G T N O J
A P A P S I E R R A K M E X M E H L V S
L L R M K F X W O O D N U D R O G I E F
P E N G A O H R E C H O Q O T D Y R M D
H A Z K E R L M O G N A T E S T N Y B K
A V J R B M O A B A H C L O E C M L E X
S U E M V R I J D D I J I V R Z A P R V
R M X Z K K A K N V N W M L Q T L R V G
A G F R G U I V E Y D F A A E T X R A Y
J Z F O X Z J L O O I Q N A T Y U O T P
J U L I E T Z Y Q W A Y V P A H W R F Q
K F W H I S K Y Y A N K E E E Q I G Q Z
```

133

# Page 58: Music and Movies Crossword

|   |   | ¹L | I | G | ²H | T | Y | E | A | R |   |
|---|---|---|---|---|---|---|---|---|---|---|---|
|   | ³C |   |   |   | A |   |   |   |   |   |   |
|   | O |   | ⁴E | R | E | A | D | E | R | ⁵R |
|   | M |   |   |   | R |   |   |   |   | E |   |
|   | P |   |   |   | Y |   | ⁶I |   |   | C |   |
| ⁷H | A | R | D |   | P |   | N |   |   | O |   |
|   | C |   |   |   | O |   | F |   |   | R |   |
|   | ⁸T | O | Y | S | T | O | R | Y |   | D |   |
|   |   |   |   |   | T |   | A |   |   |   |   |
|   |   |   |   |   | E |   | R |   |   |   |   |
| ⁹A | ¹⁰V | A | T | A | R |   | E |   |   |   |   |
|   | I |   |   |   |   |   | D |   |   |   |   |
| ¹¹E | D | I | S | O | N |   |   |   |   |   |   |
|   | E |   |   |   |   |   |   |   |   |   |   |
| ¹²W | O | O | D | Y |   |   |   |   |   |   |   |

134

# Page 69: Internet Wordsearch

```
H G P X R K Q K V S B N U K B Z K A K
B R O W S E R H O F A E W P J S T J W
P I I O L A T E E P B O W W N Q U H X
A Q X I G D Q U S I S B O S E S C U Z
X P N P I L R A O Q A R I N E D O N A
Z K M M Z T E O Z R L T I R L R O Y O
E W E B S I T E R D X Q V I Q W N N T
A E R Q F W H G W E R E J N O E U S S
R B B C V X F I T Q R I L G T W W W O
P P W T L B D R K V P X N W G W A G H
A A Y J F E E T C Q Y Y O U T U B E T
N G U U W P V I N F O R M A T I O N T
E E Y E Y S Y V D E K S R M H R F R P
T D B H G O P C Y K O O B E C A F U O
```

# Page 75: Egypt's Ruler

**Q.** Who ruled Egypt from 2589 to 2566 BC?

**A.** Khufu, better known as Cheops.

# Page 80: Quick Email Quiz

1(c). 2(c). 3(b). 4(a). 5(c).

# Picture Credits

# Thanks to:

Gaby Morgan and all at Macmillan Children's Books, who continue to offer their help and support.

Wendy Burford, Dan Albert and Charlotte Connelly at the Science Museum, London, and Tom Woolley at the National Media Museum – thanks for setting me straight as I ambled into unfamiliar techno-territory. Your comments and suggestions were all much appreciated. Thanks also to Mark Steed for keeping calm under fire and handling the last-minute Science Museum events with aplomb. Cheers, man!

Dr Eddie Grant and Dr Min Ki Lee of the North Carolina State University Center for Robotics and Intelligent Machines – I hugely enjoyed talking with you both, and your insights and predictions for the future of robotics made this book at least twice as interesting as it would have been.

Jennifer Weston at NCSU for making the above conversations possible!

Michael C. Harris of Rockwell Automation – your descriptions of industrial robots and the basics of robot movement and programming were a big help – thanks so much for taking the time to chat.

Jeff Shearer, also of Rockwell Automation, for helping with the above and for being an all-round top bloke.

Jimmy Lee at Innvo Labs for sending me my very own Pleo!

Henry Walker and all the staff and pupils of the Carolina Friends School. Once again you were an inspiration to me in finishing this book.

Helen (Crewella) and Belle for Pleo-rescue services above and beyond the call of duty. Was great to meet you both!

As always, to the Murphs, the Witts and all our family and friends . . .

. . . and to Heather, Sean, Ka-ge and Austin – it's nice to go away, but it's so much nicer to come home.

# SPACE

## THE WHOLE
## WHIZZ-BANG STORY

WHAT IS THE UNIVERSE?
WHAT WOULD HAPPEN IF YOU WERE FLYING
A SPACESHIP NEAR A BLACK HOLE?
HOW DO WE KNOW THAT STARS AND GALAXIES
ARE BILLIONS OF YEARS OLD?

GLENN MURPHY ANSWERS THESE AND A LOT OF OTHER BRILLIANT
QUESTIONS IN THIS FUNNY AND INFORMATIVE BOOK.

PACKED WITH INFORMATION, PUZZLES, QUIZZES, PHOTOS
AND DOODLES ABOUT ALL SORTS OF INCREDIBLE THINGS
LIKE SUPERMASSIVE BLACK HOLES, GALAXIES, TELESCOPES,
PLANETS, SOLAR FLARES, CONSTELLATIONS, ECLIPSES AND RED
DWARFS, THIS BOOK HAS NO BORING BITS!

By me,
GLENN MURPHY